The Elder Edda:
A Selection

The Elder Edda
A Selection

☆

TRANSLATED FROM THE ICELANDIC BY
PAUL B. TAYLOR AND W. H. AUDEN

INTRODUCTION BY
PETER H. SALUS & PAUL B. TAYLOR
NOTES BY
PETER H. SALUS

FABER AND FABER
London

First published in 1969
First published in this edition 1973
by Faber and Faber Limited
3 Queen Square London WC1
Printed in Great Britain by
Whitstable Litho
Straker Brothers Ltd.
All rights reserved

ISBN 0 571 10319 7 (Faber Paper Covered Editions)
ISBN 0 571 09066 4 (hard bound edition)

For
J.R.R. Tolkien

Acknowledgments

We would like to thank the editors of
the Windhover Press (University of Iowa); the
New York Review of Books; *The Quest*; *The Massachusetts Review*; and *The Atlantic Monthly*
where various of these poems first appeared.
We wish also to express our thanks to Professor
James E. Cathey of the University of Massachusetts
for his aid on textual and lexical matters.
Mr. Taylor's work was facilitated by a grant from
the National Translation Centre, Austin, Texas.
The drawings on pp. 164 and 172 are by Miss Elizabeth Cooper-Reive.

Contents

Introduction

The Old Icelandic Poetic Tradition

Icelandic traditional poetry finds its origin in oral composition long before the art of writing was known or used in Scandinavia to record poetic texts. The poetry is traditional in the sense that it was transmitted by oral performance, and survived for centuries, passed from generation to generation, by oral transmission. There is no question of authorship, for the poet (*fornskáld*) was a performer rather than an originator. He recounted familiar material and his performance of a particular story differed from other performances in metrical and lexical interpretation. Two versions of the story of Atli's death (Attila the Hun) appear in the heroic poems of the *Edda*, one told economically, the other with an abundance of detail. Not until poetry was recorded in manuscript, most likely during the thirteenth century, was there a sense of a unique copy or of an 'authentic' version.

On the other hand, alongside eddaic, or traditional poetry, there existed a poetic tradition formal in character and individual in composition. This tradition is known as skaldic poetry, after the Icelandic word for poet — *skáld*. While the meter and diction of eddaic poetry are relatively simple, skaldic verse is composed in a variety of complex forms and employs a larger number of involved metaphors, or *kenningar*.

Old Icelandic traditional poetry appears to have derived from the same common Germanic stock as Old High German, Old English, and Old Saxon poetry. It shares the same verse line, known generally as the long alliterative line. It

13

shares, apparently, the same lexical inventory, the same stereotyped diction. For example, the formula *firar í fólki* 'warriors among the folk', which appears in 'The Treachery of Asmund', occurs in the Old High German *Hildebrandslied* (*fireo in folche*) and in the Old English riddles (*firum on folce*), although the forms in which these poems appear suggest that their dates of composition span half a millennium. The similarity of meter and repetition of diction throughout the Germanic poetic traditions are evidences of the striking stability of traditional poetry, even before writing 'fixed' such forms.

The materials of the Germanic traditions are also comparable. The heroes of Icelandic heroic legends participate in the same events and belong to the same historical milieu as the heroes of Old High German and Old English heroic poetry. Old Icelandic poetry is unique, however, in the manner in which it treats traditional Germanic gods. There are only scant references and allusions to the Germanic pagan pantheon in Old English Chronicles and genealogies. Possibly the early arrival of Christianity in England— first with the converted Romans during the last years of the Empire's occupation, and then with the Celtic monasteries, and finally with the proselytizing Roman Catholic Church during the sixth century A.D. — seems to have inhibited the continuation of whatever poetic tradition might have existed about the older gods. Both Old English and Old High German traditional poetry successfully adapted their techniques to the incorporation of Christian materials, while the Old Icelandic tradition seems never to have been able to incorporate the new materials, except in a few isolated later literary imitations of the traditional form. The reason for this difference in development lies undoubtedly with the late arrival of Christianity in Scandinavia (A.D. 1000), and the paucity of foreign clergy in Iceland before the fourteenth century. Traditional myths appear to have been very popular in Iceland for three centuries after the conversion, while comparable poetry was being forcibly suppressed on the Continent and in the British Isles. Further, poetry as entertainment was obviously tolerated and encouraged in Iceland at a time when arts in Christian Europe were directed toward revelation of Scripture and declaration of Church doctrine. Of course, the lack of a substantial number of foreign clergy in Iceland prevented the literate decay — or corruption — of the Icelandic language that would have resulted from competition with the more acceptable language of Christian culture — Latin. The vernacular remained a rich means of literary expression and developed to a greater extent than elsewhere in Europe, with the possible exception of England under the enlightened King Alfred. Into Icelandic were translated French romances and Latin Chronicles. The thirteenth-century Icelander could read in his own language the romances of *Le Chevalier au Lion*, the legends of Merlin and Arthur, and the history of Charlemagne.

Icelandic traditional poetry differs from the other Germanic traditions in several other respects as well. First, the poetry falls syntactically into stanzas, or strophes, while the rest of Germanic traditional verse, with very few exceptions, is stichic; that is, without strophic division and with a considerable amount of emjambment, which is absent in the Icelandic. Second, eddaic poetry uses dialogue to a larger extent that either Old English or Old High German poetry. There is, proportionally, little poetic narrative in the Old Icelandic corpus. However, in place of narrative description there are frequently prose narrative links at the head or the foot of poems and even interpolated between strophes. These suggest either degeneration of older poetic narrative passages or a late editor's attempt to make clear a dramatic

15

situation obscured by the economy of the verse. One must remember, however, that the intended audience of the poetry was familiar with the poet's material. No traditional performer would dream of trying to be 'original' in selecting material. His audience expected the old 'true' stories, and not 'made-up' ones, but awaited the skáld's personal inventions in dialogue. The mythological allusions which to the modern reader seem obscure and remote, must have been suggestive to the audience and readers of the thirteenth century. So the poetic performance could afford to be economical. It suggested rather than described the details of incidents.

Performance of traditional poems did not depend on dramatic suspense, since the audience was expected to know the outcome of the story anyway. The poet could, however, play on his audience's anticipation of the manner in which the inevitable was to come about. So, for example, in the heroic poems three different versions of the manner of Sigurd's death are offered in three separate poems. The fact of Sigurd's death could not be altered, but one could vary the details of *how* death comes.

Traditional Icelandic poetry also contains a good deal of what may be called 'courtesy-book' materials; that is, instruction relating to domestic and heroic rituals of everyday life. The same sort of materials appear in the Old English poetic *Maxims*, and in the Finnish *Kalevala*. Such an interest is evidence of how close these poetic traditions were to the priestly tradition of moral instruction from which these aphoristic guides to a good life probably derive.

Prosody

A reader brought up on English poetry since Chaucer — or, for that matter, on Greek and Latin poetry — may at first have some difficulty in 'hearing' Icelandic verse, for he will find nothing he can recognize as a metrical foot, that is to say, a syllabic unit containing a fixed number of syllables with a fixed structure of either (as in English) stressed and unstressed syllables or (as in Greek and Latin) long and short syllables.

In English verse, lines are metrically equivalent only if they contain both the same kind of feet, and the same number of syllables. But in Icelandic verse, as in Anglo-Saxon, all lines are metrically equivalent which contain the same number of stressed syllables: the unstressed syllables preceding or succeeding these may vary between none and three (occasionally more).

The principal meters in Icelandic poetry are two: Epic Meter (*fornyrðislag*: 'old verse') and Chant Meter (*ljoða- háttr*).

EPIC METER

This is essentially the same as the meter of *Beowulf*. Each line contains four stresses and is divided by a strongly marked caesura into two half-lines with two stresses each. (In printing Icelandic verse, the convention has been to leave a gap between the two half-lines: in our translations we have printed the whole line as it is normally printed in an English poem.)

The two half-lines are linked by alliteration. The first stressed syllable of the second half-line must alliterate with either or both of the stressed syllables in the first: its second stressed syllable must not alliterate.

All vowels are considered to alliterate with each other. In the case of syllables beginning with *s*, *sc* (*sk*) can only alliterate with *sc*, *sh* with *sh*, and *st* with *st* etc.: similarly, voiced and unvoiced *th* can only alliterate with themselves.

17

In Icelandic poetry, unlike Anglo-Saxon, the lines are nearly always end-stopped without enjambment, and are grouped into strophes varying in length from two to six or seven lines, the commonest strophe having four.

> Depárt! You sháll not páss through
> My táll gátes of tówering stóne:
> It befíts a wífe to wínd yárn,
> Nót to knów anóther's húsband.

CHANT METER

The unit is a couplet, the first of which is identical with the standard line of Epic Meter: the second contains three stresses instead of four (some hold that it only contains two), two of which must be linked by alliteration.

> If you knów a fáithful fríend you can trúst,
> Gó óften to his hóuse:
> Gráss and brámbles grów quíckly
> Upón an untródden tráck.

SPEECH METER AND INCANTATION METER

Though these are officially classified as separate meters, they are better thought of as variations on Epic Meter and Chant Meter respectively. There is no case of a poem written entirely in either, nor even of a long sustained passage within a poem.

In Speech Meter (*málaháttr*), each half-line contains an extra stress, making six in all.

> Líttle it ís to dený, lóng it ís to trável

In Incantation Meter (*kviðuháttr*), two couplets of Chant Meter are followed by a fifth line of three stresses, which is a verbal variation on the fourth line.

18

> I know a tenth: if troublesome ghosts
>> Ride the rafters aloft,
> I can work it so they wander astray,
>> Unable to find their *forms*,
>> Unable to find their *homes*.

QUANTITY

In Icelandic verse, vowel length plays a role, though by no means as important a one as in Greek and Latin. For example, if a line ends in a single stressed syllable (a masculine ending), this may be either short or long: but if it ends in a disyllable, the first of which is stressed (a feminine ending), the stressed syllable must be short. For example, *Ever* would be permissible: *Evil* would not.

Icelandic, like Greek and Latin, is an inflected language: modern English has lost nearly all its inflections. This means that, in modern English, vowels which are short in themselves are always becoming long by position, since, more often than not, they will be followed by more than one consonant. For example, in the line

> Of Man's first disobedience, and the fruit

there is, if it is scanned quantitatively, only one short syllable, *dis*.

Quantitative verse, as Robert Bridges has demonstrated, *can* be written in English, but only as a virtuoso feat. In our translations, therefore, we have ignored quantity. Also now and again, though actually very seldom, we have ignored the strong caesura between the two half-lines, when it seemed more natural to do so.

The Kenning

The kennings so common in Icelandic poetry are, like the epithets in Homer, metrical formulae but, unlike the latter,

19

their meaning is not self-evident. *Diomedes of the loud war-cry* is a straightforward description, but no reader can guess that *Grani's Road* means the river Rhine, unless he already knows the Volsung legend in which Grani is the name of Sigurd's horse. The kenning may be exemplified by such usages as 'Meiti's plain' for the sea or 'Meiti's slopes' for the waves: Meiti was one of the sea-gods and thus stands in the same relationship to the sea as other gods stand to the land or the mountains. Other kennings are based on allusion to a mythological event: Odin was once hanged himself — see the 'Words of the High One' — he is therefore the 'gallow's load'; the Nibelung's treasure was submerged in the Rhine and all gold glitters, therefore gold can be called 'Rhine fire, or 'Rhine gravel'. In later verse the kennings become most complicated. For example, falconry caused 'hawk's land' to become a kenning for 'arm'. The wearing of arm-rings of gold caused 'gold' to be called 'arm-fire'. These were then combined so that 'hawk's land's flame' means 'gold', etc.

The Riddles and Charms

Poetic composition of riddles was principally an exercise of scholastic wit throughout the Middle Ages. Hundreds of Latin riddles in poetic form have survived. In general they are puzzles in which some object or phenomenon is described; the reader or listener is expected to 'solve' the puzzle and state the object. Riddle-making was equally popular in the vernacular. In Old English, for example, almost a hundred survive.

The lack of a Latin-educated clergy in Iceland accounts for the non-existence of such a tradition there, but a similar type of riddle does appear in Old Icelandic poetry. In the *Heidreks saga*, Odin disguises himself as Gestumblindi and challenges the king to guess his riddles, all of which are

elaborate metaphors for common things. Since Odin knows
the answers himself, the whole affair is a sport, a rather
elaborate parlor game. But, when Gestumblindi tires of the
sport he asks a question of Heidrek, the answer to which no
one can know except Odin: 'What said Odin in the ear of
Baldur before he was carried to the fire?' The same question
ends his battle of wits with Vafthruthnir, and the loser of
such a challenge has usually wagered his head. A sort of
riddle occurs in the *Halfs saga* poem 'The Treachery of
Asmund' in the dreams of Innstein. Half fails to guess the
true portent of the dreams (or, more likely, is too bold to be
prudent even though he suspects ill of his host), and is sub-
sequently killed. The riddles of Gestumblindi and the
dreams of Innstein are puzzles demanding a correct in-
terpretation. They appeal to a process of thought rather
than to an inventory of knowledge.

The riddles in the mythological poems of the *Edda* are of a
different character and appear to serve a different function.
The questions Thor poses of Alvis, and Alvis' subsequent
replies, make up a textbook of poetic diction for common
things in each world. The purpose of the inquisition,
outside of the immediate dramatic situation in which Thor
guards a goddess by keeping a dwarf at bay, is mnemonic.
The poetic structure preserves, and makes memorable,
poetic synonyms for important vocabulary items. Such em-
phasis on the *mot juste* for a thing, according to the speaker
is an example of Germanic name-magic, associated with the
primitive belief that knowledge of the proper name for a
thing gives the knower the ability to evoke the object, or its
power. There is a saga incident in which several Icelanders,
floundering in a small boat at sea, want to pray for deliver-
ance from their peril, but they have to seek someone who
knows the name of God. Once he is found, they are saved.

'The Lay of Vafthrudnir' is also mnemonic, but an

exposition of myth rather than a lexicon. The riddles, or questions, in the poem, however, are pertinent to the dramatic situation as well. Challenging an opponent with riddles is a means whereby Odin can coerce giants and the dead to reveal more of their wisdom than they would wish to, especially if they knew who their inquisitor was. Odin must disguise himself so that the challenge will be accepted. Odin searches for knowledge of the fate of the gods, so his questioning leads toward revelation of the future, though it begins with asking for exposition of the past. Proper questioning — that is, ritual questioning — functions like a charm. It compels response unless the questioned person does not know the answer, in which case the inquisition ends. This is, in a sense, Odin's security, for he can end the challenge at any point by asking the unanswerable question.

Riddles also suggest the Nordic fascination with the apparent relationship between the structure of language and the structure of the cosmos. For the Scandinavians the wisest man — he who knows most of the structure of the cosmos — is also the most skilful poet. It is, hence, appropriate that the god who is compelled to search out the facts of the cosmogonic scheme is the god of poetry. Before Odin, the giants possessed the mead of poetry, and the giants still have knowledge unknown to the gods. They can, for example, remember a time when the gods did not yet exist, and they must, therefore, have been present at the birth of language. Knowing the name of something and knowing the events of the past imply some control over the future. There is in the Nordic mind a subtle relationship, and a necessary one, between an event and the language with which it is described or anticipated. Questions and answers, then, seek to put into a harmonious relationship man's thought and the facts of the world about him which he cannot fully comprehend or control.

Charms, as T. S. Eliot so nicely puts it in *The Music of Poetry*, 'are very practical formulae designed to produce definite results, such as getting a cow out of a bog'. Charms derive from priestly incantations which solicited gods and forces of nature to fulfil their roles in turning the wheel of seasons. By the time priestly incantation transformed into poetry, and poetry found a means of being recorded in manuscript, charms had developed into ritual accompaniment for the warrior on the battlefield as well as domestic tool in the home. Charms render weapons more efficient and a hero's courage more resolute. Charms are the healer's accompaniment in the fabrication and application of remedies for wounds and disease.

The Old Icelandic word for charm is *galdr*, associated with the verb *gala* 'to sing, to chant'. They are extant in Old High German (*galtar*) and Old English (*galdor*), but references to charms are more plentiful in the literature of Iceland and Finland, where magic continued to influence domestic life and thought for centuries after the arrival of the Christian Church. Charms in Ireland and Wales seem to have degenerated into curses and insults after the arrival of Christianity and there are comparable curses and insults in the flyting episodes of Old Icelandic heroic poetry, where exchange of words between antagonists before a battle seems to have lost its character of evoking divine assistance in favour of heaping imprecations.

Charms exist intact in Icelandic only in runes — the pre-Christian Germanic form of writing. Runes ('mysteries, secrets') are magic signs whose individual shape, or *stafr* (English *stave*), represents an incantation — that is, a charm itself. Runes are not a practical form of writing, but priestly inscription for divination or sortilege. Odin learns effective charms in the form of runes in 'The Words of the High One', and each rune (there are normally sixteen runes

23

in the Scandinavian runic 'alphabet') is associated intrinsic-
ally with a particular charm. Odin's first charm, for
example, is a 'Help' charm, and Help-charms may be
associated with the N-rune, which represents the word
Nauðr 'Need'. If one scratched this rune (ᚾ) on a finger-
nail, it should evoke aid for a particular distress. N-rune charms
seem to have been used especially for delayed child-birth.

For Odin, it appears, achieving knowledge of charms con-
sists merely in learning runes, rather than in learning the
incantations associated with each rune. Incantations are
still extant in Old English and Old High German but they no
longer exist in Old Icelandic poetry. Runic inscriptions, how-
ever, survive in great numbers in Scandinavia, usually as
inscriptions on stone grave-markers (there are over two
thousand in Sweden alone). These are evidence of a tradi-
tional association between runic charms and an intent to
protect the dead. The Christian Church officially dis-
approved of the use of runes because of their suggestion of
pagan religious practices. Runes were outlawed for some
time in Iceland and their practitioners were punished as
witches. Some grave-markers have both roman and runic
letters, as if the inscriber was assuring success by appealing
to both pagan and Christian powers.

The function of runic charms in Old Icelandic poetry
varies. Some charms, probably older than the others in
origin, directly solicit forces of nature. Charms for delayed
birth, for example, demand nature to fulfil itself. Odin's
ninth charm calms waves and winds so that seamen may
return safely to shore. His second charm, for healers, seeks
to improve the body's resistance to infection and pain. These
may be classified as domestic charms, and their lineal
descendants seem to be popular medicinal recipes.

Odin also knows charms for the battlefield, such as those
which protect against the weapons of others. Odin's third

charm blunts his enemies' weapons, and his fourth gives him power to escape fetters. His seventh protects his companions from the fires of opponents (burning others within a hall or house was considered the worst of heroic behavior, and is the cruel culmination of the feuds involving the family of Njal in *Njals saga*. Asmund fires the hall in which his guests sleep in 'The Treachery of Asmund'). Such charms are often anti-charms, for swords, if made of iron, were already considered charmed.

Besides these beneficial charms, Odin knowns another kind of magic, *seid* 'sorcery, magic', which is used to bring misfortune upon another. His tenth charm, which keeps spirits from their proper resting place, is an example. His sixteenth charm, a form of love-magic to deceive a desirable girl, is undoubtedly a form of *seid* as well.

Evocation of the dead involves still another kind of magic, known as *ergi*, 'unnaturalness, filth'. This power can be used to transform oneself (and Odin is a notorious shape-changer) or to bring about unnatural behavior in another, such as cowardice or homosexuality. Odin's twelfth charm, reviving the dead which hang from the gallows, seems to be *ergi* (a filth-rune). Skirnir, in 'Skirnir's Ride', threatens Gerd with *ergi* if she will not submit herself to Frey. Though other threats have failed, this one frightens her into submission, for she knows that *ergi* can transform her so that she will ever be loathsome to men, or so that her lust for men will be unnatural.

The Nordic Pantheon

Snorri Sturlason, Icelandic poet and historian at the turn of the twelfth century, offers an euhemeristic explanation for the origin of the northern gods in his *Ynglingasaga*: 'Far to the east of the river Don in Asia was a land called Asaland or Asaheim, whose chief city was called Asgard. In that city was a chief called Odin. It was a great center for sacrifice. Twelve priests of the temple, as the custom went, directed the sacrifices and judged between men. They were called gods (*díar* an Irish loan-word) or lords (*drótnar*); everyone paid them service and veneration'. Snorri goes on to say that Odin was so wise in counsel and so skilful in magic that people began to call his name in times of trouble, and after his death they worshipped him as a god. In his *Gylfaginning*, an exposition of traditional Icelandic myths, Snorri states that there are twelve divine gods, and then goes on to list thirteen: Odin, Thor, Baldur, Njörd, Frey, Tyr, Bragi, Heimdal, Höd (or Hödur), Vidar, Váli, Ull, and Forseti. Odin had two brothers, Vili and Vé, who qualify as gods, and there is also Aegir, god of the sea. There are many goddesses, but the only ones who play important roles in surviving myths are Freya, daughter of Njörd and sister of Frey; Frigg, Odin's wife whose name and function suggest that she was originally the same goddess as Freya; and Idun, Bragi's wife and guardian of the magic apples which restore youth to the gods. Snorri adds that many also count Loki among the gods, for he is friend and companion of Thor and foster brother to Odin, though both of his parents were giants. Both Odin and Thor had at least one giant parent as well. Loki is distinguished from the rest of the gods historically by not having any cult or place-names in Scandinavia attributable to him — and for good reason. He is a malicious shape and sex changer who had not only begotten monsters such as Fenris-wolf and the Midgard-Serpent, but had borne Odin's eight-footed horse Sleipnir. It is Loki, according to most versions of the myth, who instigated the murder of Baldur by persuading Baldur's blind brother Höd to cast a mistletoe dart at him. For this deed the other gods caught Loki, bound him to a rock and caused venom to drip on his face. There he is to stay until Ragnarök, or destruction-of-the-gods. There is an apparent analogy here to the myth of Prometheus, even to the extent that Loki's name suggests 'fire' (*lógi*). 'The Song of the Sybil' and 'Loki's Flyting' allude to these events.

Odin is the foremost of the gods. He is known by many names, among which are All-Father, High One, Father of the Slain, and the Hooded One. The latter appellation refers to his many disguises in his journeys throughout the worlds to learn of the fates of the gods. He is the god of poetry, and god of the dead. Odin achieved wisdom for the gods by acquiring the lore of runes during a ritual self-sacrifice, hanging for nine days and nights. From the giants he stole the mead of poetry. Both of these events are alluded to in 'The Words of the High One'. Because of his self-sacrifice, Odin is known also as the god of the hanged, or of the gallows. His twelfth runic charm has the power, for example, to revive the dead on the gallows so that he may speak with them. He is the god of the battle-dead as well, and hence is master of the Valkyries (Choosers of the Slain) who bring to Valhalla heroes Odin has designated to die on the battle-field. 'The Lay of Erik' describes the preparation of Valhalla in anticipation of the arrival of Erik Blood-Axe and the other chieftains killed with him at the battle of Stainmore in 954. Odin can also summon the dead from their graves and compel them to utter their wisdom. The Sybil in 'Baldur's Dreams' is such an example, forced by charms to arise from her grave. Odin is also *galdrsfaðir* 'Father-of-Charms', and his powers include *seid*, or black magic, which brings misfortune to its object. Odin is deceptive and an oath-breaker; it is said that his breaking of oaths sworn to the giants brings about the wars leading to the gods' final destruction. Therefore, Odin was popular among certain viking chieftains whose truces and solemn oaths were never meant to be held.

27

Appropriately Odin is frequently associated with beasts of battle — the raven and the wolf.

Thor is the mightiest of the gods and the only god about whom no evil can be said. He is the only one of the gods able to withstand and repel Loki. Loki's only taunt against Thor is to remind him of an incident during Thor's journey to the east when he was deceived by a giant of prodigious magical powers. The taunt is hollow, however, for Thor had acquitted himself so well during that trip that the race of giants feared for their lives. Thor is the protector of the gods against all their enemies, specifically dwarves, elves, giants, trolls, and the Midgard-Serpent. At Ragnarök he battles the Midgard-Serpent to the death. He is killer of the giants Geirrod, Hungnir, Thrym, and Hymir; and, in an ironic inversion of roles, he defeats the dwarf Alvis in a battle of wits.

Njörd and Frey are not properly *Aesir* (divine gods) at all, but *Vanir*, who had come to Asgard as hostages after a war between the *Aesir* and the *Vanir* over the question of which of the two races should demand worship. The Aesir rendered as hostages in return Mímir and Haenir. Njörd is the male counterpart of the Germanic goddess Nerthus, mentioned by Tacitus as the object of fertility rites on an island in the north. His role in the Nordic pantheon is not entirely distinct from that of his son Frey, whom, it is said, was begotten by Njörd on his own sister. Frey is one of the three principal gods of the pantheon (with Odin and Thor) in the religious cults of Scandinavia as well as in the poetry, for all of the mythological poems we possess feature one of these three gods. Frey is a fertility god. His idol at Uppsala was described as having a huge phallus. He seems to have been especially popular in certain valleys and plains of Iceland which were thought to be particularly propitious. The single myth about him that survives in the traditional poetry

28

'Skirnir's Ride', may easily be interpreted as an allegory of the impregnation of the earth with fertile grain. He is associated with the bear, and his name is apparently the source of the Old English appellation for Lord (Christ and God), *Frea*.

One other god deserves special notice. He is Baldur, the slain god, known as the purest of the gods. His death is the first catastrophe in a series of events which resolve in the destruction of the gods. Baldur, however, we are told in 'The Song of Sybil', will rise again. His death and resurrection are inevitably associated with the death and resurrection of Christ, but there is no real reason to assume direct borrowing from Christianity in the myth, for Baldur, like Adonis, is a typical sacrificial god whose myth grows out of an artful mimicry of the cyclical regeneration of the earth.

The semi-deity Völund, identified explicitly as Lord of the Elves, does not seem to have any particular elfish characteristics himself. He is the archetypal smith, like the Finnish Ilmarinen and the Greek Hephaestus. Many Germanic heroes, including Beowulf, carry swords said to be forged by Völund (English *Weland* or *Wayland*). His adventures on Nidud's island, and his apparent escape by means of hand-wrought wings, are reminiscent of the myth of Daedalus. Icelanders themselves had long ago made this comparison, for the Icelandic word for labyrinth is *völundarhús* (Völund's house).

Goddesses generally play a very minor role in the poetry, though in the heroic poems women such as Brunhild and Gudrun play very central roles. Freya is prominent in 'The Lay of Thrym'. She is demanded by Thrym as ransom for Thor's hammer, without which the gods cannot be defended. Freya indignantly refuses to sacrifice her reputation by accompanying Loki to Jötunheim (Land of the Giants), and Thor himself must masquerade as the goddess. Freya is

Njörd's daughter and known as a goddess of fertility, equivalent in the Nordic pantheon to Venus. She too is one of the Vanes, who, it seems, were all fertility gods.

Cosmology

In 'The Song of the Sybil' it is said that in the beginning there was nothing but a 'yawning gap'. The Sybil herself, however, says that she knows of nine worlds, and Vafthrudnir the giant claims that he has seen nine worlds. The poetry refers to the gods' construction of Midgard, and the raising of the temple in Asgard. The term Midgard (Middle World) implies to Snorri a tricentric structure of the universe with Asgard in the center, Midgard about it, and Utgard (Outer World) as the third ring. Utgard, we must assume further, contains Jötunheim (Land of the Giants), Alfheim (Land of the Elves), Svartalfheim (Land of the Dark Elves), and perhaps Vanaheim (Land of the Vanes). Somewhere below this structure is Niflheim, the realm of the goddess Hel. The ninth world may be that of the dwarves, but its proper name and its specific location are uncertain. Asgard, the world of the gods, and Midgard, the world of man, are protected from Utgard by a large body of water in which swims the Midgard-Serpent, so huge that he encircles all Midgard and clasps his tail in his mouth. Asgard and Midgard are connected to each other by a bridge Bifröst (Rainbow) which is said to span the water. It is across this bridge that the enemies of the gods will fare at Ragnarök. The world-ash Yggdrasil has one of its three roots embedded in Asgard, the second in Utgard, and the third in Niflheim. Under the first root is the spring of Urd (Future, or Fate; Old English *Wyrd*, Shakespeare's *weird* as in the weird sisters of Macbeth), under the second is the well of Mímir, Odin's source of wisdom, and under the third is the spring Hvergelmir, source of all rivers. The dragon Nidhögg (Deep-Biter) gnaws at the deepest root, and above four dwarves (North, South, East and West) support the sky. Two wolves pursue the sun and moon, and will catch and swallow them at Ragnarök.

Utgard must be a completely mountainous and cold region. Frost giants, mountain giants and rock elves live there. Jötunheim must be northward from Asgard, since the north is traditionally the land of death and the land of man's enemies. The trolls, presumably, live in the east or north-east, for Thor is frequently described as being 'in the east, fighting trolls'. Hel is also somewhat to the north as well as downward, since Snorri's *Gylfaginning* tells how Hérmod rode after Baldur to Hel, 'deep and to the north'. To the south lies Muspellheim (the Realm of Fire). It is difficult to say how much the Icelandic concept of Hel was influenced by the mountainous and volcanic character of Iceland, but the dimension of depth is suggested elsewhere in poetic descriptions. In 'The Lay of Grimnir' Odin looks out over the world from his throne, or high seat, Hlidskjálf (Hall of Many Doors). Frey sees down into Jötunheim from Hlidskjálf in 'Skirnir's Ride'. Whether Odin or any occupant of Hlidskjálf can see over the world just because the seat is high, or because Odin's home has certain magic properties is uncertain. As we are told that the occupant of Hlidskjálf can 'see out over all the worlds', we have placed Asgard on the edge of the universe, rather than in the center (where Snorri seems to place it, cf. pp. 164 and 172).

The dramatic situation in each of the mythological poems involves a movement between worlds, and often suggests descents from one plane to another. In 'The Song of the Sybil' Odin has journeyed downward to Niflheim to charm the Sybil into speech. 'The Lay of Vafthruthnir' is a quest into Jötunheim not only to test the giant's wit, but to learn of the impending fate of the gods. 'The Lay of Grimnir' is ostensibly a quest to test human virtue, but it turns into an exposition of Odin's wit, as well as a revelation of his pseudonyms. 'Skirnir's Ride' is Frey's quest for a bride in Jötunheim, and Thor quests for a giant kettle in 'The Lay of Hymir' in which to brew beer for the gods' feast. 'The Lay of Thrym' is a quest to recover from Jötunheim Thor's hammer. 'Baldur's Dreams' is another of Odin's quests to learn of the fate of the gods. 'Brunhild's Hel-Ride' tells of Brunhild's journey from Midgard to Hel as the Valkyrie seeks to follow her slain lover Sigurd (in Hel rather than in Valhalla because he was slain in bed rather than on the battlefield).

Descent into a lower world in order to acquire secrets of life and death denied living beings is a mythological archetype. Odin parallels heroes of many traditions in this respect — Gilgamesh, Ulysses, Aeneas, and Sir Guyon are but a few. Odin wins his battle of wits in such confrontations with knowers of truth, but generally fails to grasp the significance of the answers he extracts. Not until he questions the Sybil does he receive the full and explicit statement of the gods' fate.

The mythological poems of Icelandic tradition are typologically related to Nordic heroic legends in poetry. The former constitute a kind of mythological explication of the condition of universal life, and the latter illustrate struggles of men within these conditions. What happens in Asgard foreshadows what will come to pass in Midgard. As the gods struggle to prevent a destruction they know is inescapable, so heroes are implicitly urged to face inevitable fate without succumbing to despair. As the race of gods anticipates resurrection, so the heroes anticipate enduring fame. The typological association between poems of gods and poems of heroes lends them similar structures. The lays of Thrym and Völund illustrate this general correspondence. Each hero, Völund and Thor, is robbed of his most valued possession, without which each feels powerless. To regain his hammer, Thor must allow himself to be disguised as a woman; Völund, before he can regain his sword, is hamstrung. Each must journey to another world before recovering his loss, and, in each instance, recovery takes place during a kind of mock wedding. Völund weds Bodvild (whom he calls his 'bride') by assaulting her. Thor's wedding feast ends with his slaughter of the giants. Both tales echo earlier myths of regeneration.

Despite the frequent journeys of gods to Jötunheim and to Midgard, there is very little mingling of the affairs of mortals with the affairs of gods. For the most part, gods are conspicuously absent in the heroic poems, and mortals are absent from the poems about gods (except for references to men in the prose accompanying the poems). Giants never appear in Midgard, and when dwarves appear they seem to refer more to stunted humans than to the enemies of gods. Although Valhalla is an important concept in heroic life, there are no poems, other than the contrived 'Lay of Erik', that mention the presence of mortals in Asgard.

Bibliographical Note

The following notes are intended for the interested reader who wishes to delve further into Icelandic mythology, literature or history.

Scandinavian Archaeology and History

Haakon Shetelig and Hjalmar Falk, *Scandinavian Archaeology*, translated by E. V. Gordon (Oxford University Press).

Johannes Brønsted, *The Vikings* (Penguin Books).

Mythology

Peter Andreas Munch, *Norse Mythology*, revised by Magur Olsen, translated by Sigurd Bernhard Hustvedt (American-Scandinavian Foundation). Over forty years old, this book is rather staid but thorough.

H. R. Ellis Davidson, *Gods and Myths of Northern Europe* (Penguin Books).

E. O. G. Turville-Petre, *Myth and Religion of the North* (Weidenfeld and Nicolson). By far the best work on Scandinavian mythology.

Literature

W. P. Ker, *Epic and Romances* (Dover Books).

G. Turville-Petre, *Origins of Icelandic Literature* (Oxford University Press).

BIBLIOGRAPHICAL NOTE

Stefán Einarsson, *A History of Icelandic Literature* (American-Scandinavian Foundation).

Insofar as further reading in the literature itself is concerned, the various sagas available in Penguin (translated by Magnus Magnusson and Hermann Pálsson) and in Oxford World Classics (translated by Gwyn Jones) are of high quality. Concerning the sagas themselves, Theodore Andersson's *The Problems of Icelandic Saga Origins* (Yale University Press) and Peter Hallberg's *The Icelandic Saga*, translated by Paul Schach (University of Nebraska Press) are of great interest.

Textual Note

Except for 'Erik', 'Asmund' and 'Angantyr', all of the translations are based on the edition of the *Edda* as found in the *Codex Regius* of G. Neckel, as revised by Kuhn (1962). In a few places we have preferred the readings of other editions, especially that of Jón Helgason. A few lines have been taken over from the *Hauksbók* manuscript. The sources of the three non-Eddic poems are given separately.

Especially in the cases of 'Words of the High One' and 'The Song of the Sybil', we have silently rearranged some of the verses and altered, here and there, the order of the strophes — but only when it seemed to us to add to the sense of the poem.

In 'Words of the High One', for example, we have conflated some of the strophes, so that the manuscript's 165 strophes are but 157 in this version. In 'The Song of the Sybil', we have followed a suggestion of Sophus Bugge and rearranged the strophes so that our 1–4 are 22, 29, 28, 27 in the original. Further we have inserted into our strophe 33 the fragment of the manuscript's 37; transferred 41 to follow 56; added a line to 15; and omitted the manuscript's 49, 54, and 58, which are repetitions of 44. Finally, whereas in the original the Sybil speaks now in the first person, now in the third, we have made her speak in the first person throughout.

The Words of the High One

Young and alone on a long road,   *1*
    Once I lost my way:
Rich I felt when I found another;
    Man rejoices in man.

A kind word need not cost much,   *2*
    The price of praise can be cheap:
With half a loaf and an empty cup
    I found myself a friend.

Two wooden stakes stood on the plain,   *3*
    On them I hung my clothes:
Draped in linen, they looked well born,
    But, naked, I was a nobody.

Too early to many homes I came,   *4*
    Too late, it seemed, to some:
The ale was finished or else unbrewed,
    The unpopular cannot please.

Some would invite me to visit their homes,   *5*
    But none thought I needed a meal,
As though I had eaten a whole joint
    Just before with a friend who had two.

The man who stands at a strange threshold,   *6*
    Should be cautious before he cross it,
    Glance this way and that:
Who knows beforehand what foes may sit
    Awaiting him in the hall?

Greetings to the host. The guest has arrived.   7
   In which seat shall he sit?
Rash is he who at unknown doors
   Relies on his good luck.

Fire is needed by the newcomer   8
   Whose knees are frozen numb;
Meat and clean linen a man needs
   Who has fared across the fells.

Water, too, that he may wash before eating,   9
   Handcloths and a hearty welcome,
Courteous words, then courteous silence
   That he may tell his tale.

Who travels widely needs his wits about him,   10
   The stupid should stay at home:
The ignorant man is often laughed at
   When he sits at meat with the sage.

Of his knowledge a man should never boast,   11
   Rather be sparing of speech
When to his house a wiser comes:
   Seldom do those who are silent
Make mistakes; mother-wit
   Is ever a faithful friend.

A guest should be cautious when he comes to the
       table,   12
   And sit in wary silence,
His ears attentive, his eyes alert:
   So he protects himself.

Fortunate is he who is favored in his lifetime   13
   With praise and words of wisdom:

38

Evil counsel is often given
   By those of evil heart.

Better gear than good sense   *14*
   A traveler cannot carry,
Better than riches for a wretched man,
   Far from his own home.

Better gear than good sense   *15*
   A traveler cannot carry,
A more tedious burden than too much drink
   A traveler cannot carry.

Less good than belief would have it   *16*
   Is mead for the sons of men:
A man knows less the more he drinks,
   Becomes a befuddled fool.

I-forget is the name men give the heron   *17*
   Who hovers over the feast:
Fettered I was in his feathers that night,
   When a guest in Gunnlod's court.

Drunk I got, dead drunk,   *18*
   When Fjalar the Wise was with me:
Best is the banquet one looks back on after,
   And remembers all that happened.

Silence becomes the son of a Prince,   *19*
   To be silent but brave in battle:
It befits a man to be merry and glad
   Until the day of his death.

The coward believes he will live forever   *20*
   If he holds back in the battle,

But in old age he shall have no peace
    Though spears have spared his limbs.

When he meets friends, the fool gapes,   *21*
    Is shy and sheepish at first,
Then he sips his mead and immediately
    All know what an oaf he is.

He who has seen and suffered much,   *22*
    And knows the ways of the world,
He who has traveled, can tell what spirit
    Governs the men he meets.

Drink your mead, but in moderation,   *23*
    Talk sense or be silent:
No man is called discourteous who goes
    To bed at an early hour.

A gluttonous man who guzzles away   *24*
    Brings sorrow on himself:
At the table of the wise he is taunted often,
    Mocked for his bloated belly.

The herd knows its homing time,   *25*
    And leaves the grazing ground:
But the glutton never knows how much
    His belly is able to hold.

An ill-tempered, unhappy man   *26*
    Ridicules all he hears,
Makes fun of others, refusing always
    To see the faults in himself.

Foolish is he who frets at night,   *27*
    And lies awake to worry:

A weary man when morning comes,
    He finds all as bad as before.

The fool thinks that those who laugh   *28*
    At him are all his friends,
Unaware when he sits with wiser men
    How ill they speak of him.

The fool thinks that those who laugh   *29*
    At him are all his friends:
When he comes to the Thing and calls for support,
    Few spokesmen he finds.

The fool who fancies he is full of wisdom   *30*
    While he sits by his hearth at home,
Quickly finds when questioned by others
    That he knows nothing at all.

The ignorant booby had best be silent   *31*
    When he moves among other men,
No one will know what a nitwit he is
    Until he begins to talk;
No one knows less what a nitwit he is
    Than the man who talks too much

To ask well, to answer rightly,   *32*
    Are the marks of a wise man:
Men must speak of men's deeds,
    What happens may not be hidden.

Wise is he not who is never silent,   *33*
    Mouthing meaningless words:
A glib tongue that goes on chattering
    Sings to its own harm.

A man among friends should not mock another: *34*
    Many believe the man
Who is not questioned to know much
    And so he escapes their scorn.

An early meal a man should take   *35*
    Before he visits friends,
Lest, when he gets there, he go hungry,
    Afraid to ask for food.

The fastest friends may fall out   *36*
    When they sit at the banquet board:
It is, and shall be, a shameful thing
    When guest quarrels with guest.

The wise guest has his way of dealing   *37*
    With those who taunt him at table:
He smiles through the meal, not seeming to hear
    The twaddle talked by his foes.

The tactful guest will take his leave   *38*
    Early, not linger long:
He starts to stink who outstays his welcome
    In a hall that is not his own.

A small hut of one's own is better,   *39*
    A man is his master at home:
A couple of goats and a corded roof
    Still are better than begging.

A small hut of one's own is better,   *40*
    A man is his master at home:
His heart bleeds in the beggar who must
    Ask at each meal for meat.

A wayfarer should not walk unarmed,   *41*
    But have his weapons to hand:
He never knows when he may need a spear,
    Or what menace meet on the road.

No man is so generous he will jib at accepting   *42*
    A gift in return for a gift,
No man so rich that it really gives him
    Pain to be repaid.

Once he has won wealth enough,   *43*
    A man should not crave for more:
What he saves for friends, foes may take;
    Hopes are often liars.

With presents friends should please each other,   *44*
    With a shield or a costly coat:
Mutual giving makes for friendship
    So long as life goes well.

A man should be loyal through life to friends,   *45*
    To them and to friends of theirs,
But never shall a man make offer
    Of friendship to their foes.

A man should be loyal through life to friends,   *46*
    And return gift for gift,
Laugh when they laugh, but with lies repay
    A false foe who lies.

If you find a friend you fully trust   *47*
    And wish for his good will,
Exchange thoughts, exchange gifts,
    Go often to his house.

If you deal with another you don't trust
    But wish for his good will,
Be fair in speech but false in thought
    And give him lie for lie.
        48

Even with one you ill-trust
    And doubt what he means to do,
False words with fair smiles
    May get you the gift you desire.
        49

To a false friend the footpath winds
    Though his house be on the highway:
To a sure friend there is a short cut,
    Though he live a long way off.
        50

The generous and bold have the best lives,
    Are seldom beset by cares,
But the base man sees bogies everywhere,
    And the miser pines for presents.
        51

As the young fir that falls and rots,
    Having neither needles or bark,
So is the fate of the friendless man:
    Why should he live long?
        52

Little a sand-grain, little a dewdrop,
    Little the minds of men:
All men are not equal in wisdom,
    The half-wise are everywhere.
        53

It is best for man to be middle-wise,
    Not over cunning and clever:
The fairest life is led by those
    Who are deft at all they do.
        54

It is best for man to be middle-wise,   *55*
    Not over cunning and clever:
No man is able to know his future,
    So let him sleep in peace.

It is best for man to be middle-wise,   *56*
    Not over cunning and clever:
The learned man whose lore is deep
    Is seldom happy at heart.

Brand kindles brand till they burn out,   *57*
    Flame is quickened by flame:
One man from another is known by his speech,
    The simpleton by his silence.

Early shall he rise who has designs   *58*
    On another's land or life:
His prey escapes the prone wolf,
    The sleeper is seldom victorious.

Early shall he rise who rules few servants,   *59*
    And set to work at once:
Much is lost by the late sleeper,
    Wealth is won by the swift.

A man should know how many logs   *60*
    And strips of bark from the birch
To stock in autumn, that he may have enough
    Wood for his winter fires.

Washed and fed, one may fare to the Thing   *61*
    Though one's clothes be the worse for wear:
None need be ashamed of his shoes or hose,
    Nor of the horse he owns,
    Although no thoroughbred.

As the eagle who comes to the ocean shore,   *62*
   Sniffs and hangs her head,
Dumbfounded is he who finds at the Thing
   No supporters to plead his case.

It is safe to tell a secret to one,   *63*
   Risky to tell it to two,
To tell it to three is thoughtless folly,
   Everyone else will know.

Often words uttered to another   *64*
   Have reaped an ill harvest:
Two beat one, the tongue is head's bane,
   Pockets of fur hide fists.

Moderate at council should a man be,   *65*
   Not brutal and overbearing:
Among the bold the bully will find
   Others as bold as he.

These things are thought the best: *66*
   Fire, the sight of the sun,
Good health with the gift to keep it,
   And a life that avoids vice.

Not all sick men are utterly wretched:
   Some are blessed with sons,   *67*
Some with friends, some with riches,
   Some with worthy works.

The halt can manage a horse, the handless a flock,   *68*
   The deaf be a doughty fighter,
To be blind is better than to burn on a pyre:
   There is nothing the dead can do.

It is always better to be alive,   *69*
   The living can keep a cow:
Fire, I saw, warming a wealthy man,
   With a cold corpse at his door.

A son is a blessing, though born late   *70*
   To a father no longer alive:
Stones would seldom stand by the highway
   If sons did not set them there.

He welcomes the night who has enough provisions: *71*
   Short are the sails of a ship,
   Dangerous the dark in autumn,
The wind may veer within five days,
   And many times in a month.

The nitwit does not know that gold   *72*
   Makes apes of many men:
One is rich, one is poor —
   There is no blame in that.

Cattle die, kindred die,   *73*
   Every man is mortal:
But the good name never dies
   Of one who has done well.

Cattle die, kindred die,   *74*
   Every man is mortal:
But I know one thing that never dies,
   The glory of the great dead.

Fields and flocks had Fitjung's sons,   *75*
   Who now carry begging bowls:
Wealth may vanish in the wink of an eye,
   Gold is the falsest of friends.

In the fool who acquires cattle and lands, *76*
    Or wins a woman's love,
His wisdom wanes with his waxing pride,
    He sinks from sense to conceit.

Now is answered what you ask of the runes, *77*
    Graven by the gods,
    Made by the Almighty,
    Sent by the powerful sage:
It is best for man to remain silent.

For these things give thanks at nightfall: *78*
The day gone, a guttered torch,
A sword tested, the troth of a maid,
Ice crossed, ale drunk.

Hew wood in wind-time, in fine weather sail, *79*
Tell in the night-time tales to housegirls,
For too many eyes are open by day:
From a ship expect speed, from a shield cover,
Keenness from a sword, but a kiss from a girl.

Drink ale by the hearth, over ice glide, *80*
Buy a stained sword, buy a starving mare
To fatten at home: and fatten the watchdog.

Trust not an acre early sown, *81*
    Nor praise a son too soon:
Weather rules the acre, wit the son,
    Both are exposed to peril.

A snapping bow, a burning flame, *82*
A grinning wolf, a grunting boar,
A raucous crow, a rootless tree,

48

A breaking wave, a boiling kettle,
A flying arrow, an ebbing tide,
A coiled adder, the ice of a night,
A bride's bed-talk, a broad sword,
A bear's play, a Prince's children,
A witch's welcome, the wit of a slave,
A sick calf, a corpse still fresh,
A brother's killer encountered upon
The highway, a house half-burned,
A racing stallion who has wrenched a leg,
Are never safe: let no man trust them.

*　　*　　*

No man should trust a maiden's words, *83*
   Nor what a woman speaks:
Spun on a wheel were women's hearts,
   In their breasts was implanted caprice.

To love a woman whose ways are false *84*
Is like sledding over slippery ice
With unshod horses out of control,
Badly-trained two-year-olds,
Or drifting rudderless on a rough sea,
Or catching a reindeer with a crippled hand
On a thawing hillside: think not to do it.

Naked I may speak now for I know both: *85*
   Men are treacherous too.
Fairest we speak when falsest we think:
   Many a maid is deceived.

Gallantly shall he speak and gifts bring *86*
   Who wishes for woman's love:

49

Praise the features of the fair girl,
    Who courts well will conquer.

Never reproach another for his love: *87*
    It happens often enough
That beauty ensnares with desire the wise
    While the foolish remain unmoved.

Never reproach the plight of another,   *88*
    For it happens to many men:
Strong desire may stupify heroes,
    Dull the wits of the wise.

The mind alone knows what is near the heart,   *89*
    Each is his own judge:
The worst sickness for a wise man
    Is to crave what he cannot enjoy.

So I learned when I sat in the reeds,   *90*
    Hoping to have my desire:
Lovely was the flesh of that fair girl,
    But nothing I hoped for happened.

I saw on a bed Billing's daughter,   *91*
    Sun-white, asleep:
No greater delight I longed for then
    Than to lie in her lovely arms.

'Come, Odin, after nightfall   *92*
    If you wish for a meeting with me:
All would be lost if anyone saw us
    And learned that we were lovers.'

Afire with longing, I left her then,   *93*
    Deceived by her soft words:
50

I thought my wooing had won the maid,
    That I would have my way.

After nightfall I hurried back,   *94*
    But the warriors were all awake,
Lights were burning, torches blazing:
    So false proved the path.

Towards daybreak back I came.   *95*
    The guards were sound asleep:
I found then that the fair woman
    Had tied a bitch to her bed.

Many a girl when one gets to know her   *96*
    Proves to be fickle and false:
That treacherous maiden taught me a lesson,
The crafty woman covered me with shame,
    That was all I got from her.

*   *   *

Let a man with his guests be glad and merry,   *97*
    Modest a man should be,
But talk well if he intends to be wise
    And expects praise from men:
Fimbul-fambi is the fool called,
    Unable to open his mouth.

Fruitless my errand, had I been silent   *98*
    When I came to Suttung's courts:
With spirited words I spoke to my profit
    In the hall of the aged giant.

Rati had gnawed a narrow passage,   *99*
    Chewed a channel through stone,

51

A path around the roads of giants:
  I was like to lose my head.

Gunnlod sat me in the golden seat,   *100*
  Poured me precious mead:
Ill-reward she had from me for that,
  For her proud and passionate heart,
  Her brooding foreboding spirit.

What I won from her I have well used: *101*
  I have waxed in wisdom since
I came back, bringing to Asgard
  Odrerir, the sacred draught.

Hardly would I have come home alive   *102*
  From the garth of the grim troll,
Had Gunnlod not helped me, the good woman,
  Who wrapped her arms around me.

The following day the Frost Giants came,   *103*
  Walked into Har's Hall
  To ask for Har's advice:
Had Bolverk, they asked, come back to his friends
  Or had he been slain by Suttung?

Odin, they said, swore an oath on his ring: *104*
  Who from now on will trust him?
By fraud at the feast he befuddled Suttung
  And brought grief to Gunnlod.

*   *   *

It is time to sing in the seat of the wise,   *105*
  Of what at Urd's Well

I saw in silence, saw and thought on.
   Long I listened to men
   At Har's Hall,
   In Har's Hall:
   There I heard this.

Loddfafnir, listen to my counsel: *106*
   You will fare well if you follow it,
   It will help you much if you heed it.

Never rise at night unless you need to spy   *107*
   Or to ease yourself in the outhouse.

Shun a woman, wise in magic,   *108*
   Her bed and her embraces:
If she cast a spell, you will care no longer
   To meet and speak with men,
Desire no food, desire no pleasure,
   In sorrow fall asleep.

Never seduce another's wife,   *109*
   Never make her your mistress.

If you must journey to mountains and fjords,   *110*
   Take food and fodder with you.

Never open your heart to an evil man   *111*
   When fortune does not favor you:
From an evil man, if you make him your friend,
   You will get evil for good.

I saw a warrior wounded fatally   *112*
   By the words of an evil woman:
Her cunning tongue caused his death,
   Though what she alleged was a lie.

If you know a friend you can fully trust,   *113*
   Go often to his house:
Grass and brambles grow quickly
   Upon the untrodden track.

With a good man it is good to talk,   *114*
   Make him your fast friend:
But waste no words on a witless oaf,
   Nor sit with a senseless ape.

Cherish those near you, never be   *115*
   The first to break with a friend:
Care eats him who can no longer
   Open his heart to another.

An evil man, if you make him your friend,   *116*
   Will give you evil for good:
A good man, if you make him your friend,
   Will praise you in every place.

Affection is mutual when men can open   *117*
   All their heart to each other:
He whose words are always fair
   Is untrue and not to be trusted.

Bandy no speech with a bad man: *118*
   Often the better is beaten
   In a word-fight by the worse.

Be not a cobbler nor a carver of shafts,   *119*
   Except it be for yourself:
If a shoe fit ill or a shaft be crooked,
   The maker gets curses and kicks.

If aware that another is wicked, say so: *120*
   Make no truce or treaty with foes.

Never share in the shamefully gotten,   *121*
   But allow yourself what is lawful.

Never lift your eyes and look up in battle,   *122*
Lest the heroes enchant you, who can change warriors
   Suddenly into hogs.

With a good woman, if you wish to enjoy   *123*
   Her words and her good will,
Pledge her fairly and be faithful to it:
   Enjoy the good you are given.

Be not overwary, but wary enough,   *124*
   First, of the foaming ale,
Second, of a woman wed to another,
   Third, of the tricks of thieves.

Mock not the traveler met on the road,   *125*
   Nor maliciously laugh at the guest:
Scoff not at guests nor to the gate chase them,
   But relieve the lonely and wretched.

The sitters in the hall seldom know   *126*
   The kin of the newcomer:
The best man is marred by faults,
   The worst is not without worth.

Never laugh at the old when they offer counsel,   *127*
   Often their words are wise:
From shriveled skin, from scraggy things
   That hang among the hides

And move amid the guts,
Clear words often come.

Heavy the beam above the door;   *128*
   Hang a horseshoe on it
Against ill luck, lest it should suddenly
   Crash and crush your guests.

Medicines exist against many evils: *129*
Earth against drunkenness, heather against worms,
Oak against costiveness, corn against sorcery,
Spurred rye against rupture, runes against bales,
The moon against feuds, fire against sickness,
   Earth makes harmless the floods.

*   *   *

Wounded I hung on a wind-swept gallows   *130*
   For nine long nights,
Pierced by a spear, pledged to Odin,
   Offered, myself to myself:
The wisest know not from whence spring
   The roots of that ancient rood.

They gave me no bread, they gave me no mead: *131*
   I looked down; with a loud cry
I took up runes; from that tree I fell.

Nine lays of power I learned from the famous *132*
   Bolthor, Bestla's father:
He poured me a draught of precious mead,
   Mixed with magic Odrerir.

Learned I grew then, lore-wise,   *133*
   Waxed and throve well:

56

Word from word gave words to me,
Deed from deed gave deeds to me.

Runes you will find, and readable staves,   *134*
    Very strong staves,
    Very stout staves,
    Staves that Bolthor stained,
    Made by mighty powers,
    Graven by the prophetic God.

For the gods by Odin, for the elves by Dain,   *135*
    By Dvalin, too, for the dwarves,
    By Asvid for the hateful giants,
    And some I carved myself:
Thund, before man was made, scratched them,
Who rose first, fell thereafter.

Know how to cut them, know how to read them,   *136*
Know how to stain them, know how to prove them,
Know how to evoke them, know how to sacre them,
Know how to send them, know how to send them.

Better not to ask than to overpledge   *137*
    As a gift that demands a gift,
Better not to send than to slay too many.

The first charm I know is unknown to rulers   *138*
    Or any of human kind:
Help it is named, for help it can give
    In hours of sorrow and anguish.

I know a second that the sons of men   *139*
    Must learn who wish to be leeches.

I know a third: in the thick of battle,   *140*
    If my need be great enough,
It will blunt the edges of enemy swords,
    Their weapons will make no wounds.

I know a fourth: it will free me quickly   *141*
    If foes should bind me fast
With strong chains, a chant that makes
    Fetters spring from the feet,
    Bonds burst from the hands.

I know a fifth: no flying arrow,   *142*
    Aimed to bring harm to men,
Flies too fast for my fingers to catch it
    And hold it in mid-air.

I know a sixth: it will save me if a man   *143*
    Cut runes on a sapling's roots
With intent to harm; it turns the spell;
    The hater is harmed, not me.

I know a seventh: if I see the hall   *144*
    Ablaze around my bench-mates,
Though hot the flames, they shall feel nothing,
    If I choose to chant the spell.

I know an eighth: that all are glad of,   *145*
    Most useful to men:
If hate fester in the heart of a warrior,
    It will soon calm and cure him.

I know a ninth: when need I have   *146*
    To shelter my ship on the flood,
The wind it calms, the waves it smooths
    And puts the sea to sleep.

I know a tenth: if troublesome ghosts   *147*
   Ride the rafters aloft,
I can work it so they wander astray,
   Unable to find their forms,
   Unable to find their homes.

I know an eleventh: when I lead to battle   *148*
   Old comrades-in-arms,
I have only to chant it behind my shield,
   And unwounded they go to war,
   Unwounded they come from war,
   Unscathed wherever they are.

I know a twelfth: if a tree bear   *149*
   A man hanged in a halter,
I can carve and stain strong runes
   That will cause the corpse to speak,
   Reply to whatever I ask.

I know a thirteenth: if I throw a cup   *150*
   Of water over a warrior,
He shall not fall in the fiercest battle,
   Nor sink beneath the sword.

I know a fourteenth, that few know: *151*
   If I tell a troop of warriors
About the High Ones, elves and gods,
   I can name them one by one.

I know a fifteenth, that first Thjodrerir   *152*
   Sang before Delling's Doors,
Giving power to gods, prowess to elves,
   Foresight to Hroptatyr-Odin.

I know a sixteenth: If I see a girl   *153*
    With whom it would please me to play,
I can turn her thoughts, can touch the heart
    Of any white-armed woman.

I know a seventeenth: if I sing it, the young   *154*
    Girl will be slow to forsake me.

I know an eighteenth that I never tell   *155*
    To maiden or wife of man,
    A secret I hide from all
Except the love who lies in my arms,
    Or else my own sister.

To learn to sing them, Loddfafnir,   *156*
    Will take you a long time,
Though helpful they are if you understand them,
    Useful if you use them,
    Needful if you need them.

The Wise One has spoken words in the Hall,   *157*
    Needful for men to know,
    Unneedful for trolls to know:
Hail to the Speaker, hail to the Knower,
    Joy to him who has understood,
    Delight to those who have listened.

The Lay of Grimnir

King Hraudung had two sons, Agnar and Geirrod. Agnar was ten winters old and Geirrod eight when they went rowing in a boat to catch little fish. But the wind drove them out to sea. During the night they were wrecked on the shore; but they found a peasant with whom they spent the winter. The housewife cared for Agnar and the bondsman cared for Geirrod, teaching him wisdom. In the spring the peasant gave him a boat, and when the couple took the boys to the shore, the peasant spoke to Geirrod in secret. They had a fair wind and came to their father's dock. Geirrod was in the front of the boat. He leapt on to the land and pushed the boat from the shore, saying 'Go now where evil may take you!' The boat drifted out to sea. Geirrod went up to the house where he was welcomed, but his father was dead. Then Geirrod was made king and became famous.

Odin and Frigg sat in Hlidskjálf and looked over all the worlds. Odin said, 'Do you see Agnar, your foster-child, begetting children with a giantess in a cave? But Geirrod, my foster-child, is a king ruling over his land.' Frigg said, 'He is so parsimonious that he tortures his guests if he thinks there are too many of them.' Odin replied that this was a great lie; and they wagered about the truth. Frigg sent her maid, Fulla, to Geirrod. She told the king to beware otherwise a magician who had come to the land would bewitch him, and said that he could be recognized because no dog was fierce enough to leap at him. It was a great slander that Geirrod was not hospitable; but he had his men capture the man the dogs would not attack. He wore a dark-blue cloak, called himself Grimnir, and would say no more of himself, even when questioned.

61

The king had him tortured to make him speak, setting him between two fires for eight nights. King Geirrod had a son eight winters old, called Agnar after his father's brother. Agnar went to Grimnir, and gave him a full horn from which to drink, and said that the king was not right in torturing him without cause. Grimnir drank from the horn; the fire was so near that the cloak on Grimnir's back was afire. He said:

You are fierce, fire, too fierce for comfort,   *1*
    Recede from me, savage flame:
My cloak is beginning to catch fire,
    Its fur is singed and smolders.

For eight nights I have not moved,   *2*
    None offered me meat or mead
Except Agnar: the Son of Geirrod
    Shall be lord of the land of the Goths.

Hail, Agnar! The Highest One   *3*
    Bids you a grateful greeting:
For one drink your reward shall be
    Greater than any man got.

The land is hallowed that lies near   *4*
    The homes of gods and elves:
But Thor shall live in Land-of-Strength
    Till the High Ones are all destroyed.

Ull yonder in Yew-Dale   *5*
    Has made himself a mansion:
Elf-Home for Frey in the old days
    The gods gave as a tooth-fee.

The third is a bower, thatched with silver   *6*
   And built by blithe powers:
Hall of the Dead was the home chosen
   Long ago by the god.

The fourth Sunk-Bench: refreshing waves   *7*
   Sparkle and splash about it:
There Odin drinks all day with Saga,
   Glad from golden cups.

The fifth Glad-Home where, golden-bright   *8*
   The Hall of Valhalla stands:
There Hropt, the Doomer, daily chooses
   Warriors slain by weapons.

Easy to recognize for all who come there   *9*
   Is Odin's lofty hall:
With spear-shafts and shields it is roofed,
   Its benches are strewn with byrnies.

Easy to recognize for all who come there   *10*
   Is Odin's lofty hall:
The wolf lurks before the west door,
   The eagle hovers above.

The sixth Din-Home, the dwelling once   *11*
   Of Thjazi, the mighty-thewed:
Now Skadi sits in the seat of her father,
   The bright bride of gods.

The seventh Broad-Shining, where Baldur has   *12*
   Made himself a mansion,
A blessed place, the best of lands,
   Where evil runes are rare.

The eighth Heaven-Mount: Heimdal there   *13*
  Is lord of land and temple:
The gods' watchman drinks good mead,
  Glad in that peaceful place.

The ninth Battle-Plain, where bright Freya   *14*
  Decides where the warriors shall sit:
Half of the fallen follow the goddess,
  And half belong to Odin.

The tenth Glittering; it has gold pillars   *15*
  And a rich roof of silver:
There Foreseti sits as a rule
  And settles every suit.

The eleventh Harbor, where lordly Njörd   *16*
  Has made himself a mansion:
The high-timbered altar he rules,
  Peerless prince of men.

Vidar lives in the land called Wood,   *17*
  Where grass and brushwood grow:
The bold one shall leap from the back of the mare
  To avenge his father's death.

Sooty-Face in Sooty-with-Fire,   *18*
  Boils Soot-of-the-Sea:
To the Battle-slain boar's flesh
  Was ever the finest fare.

War-accustomed Warrior-Father   *19*
  Feeds it to Greedy and Grim,
For on wine alone weapon-good
  Odin always lives.

Thought and Memory each morning fly   *20*
   Over the vast earth:
Thought, I fear, may fail to return,
   But I fear more for Memory.

Thund roars fiercely, the fish of the wolf   *21*
   Frolics in the raging flood:
The river seems too rough and deep
   For the swarm of the slain to wade.

Gate-of-Dead before doors that are holy   *22*
   Stands upon hallowed acres:
Old is that gate, and how to bolt it
   Few now know.

Five hundred and forty doors   *23*
   Are built into Bilskirnir,
Furnished with rings: of roofed halls
   The largest belongs to my son.

Five hundred and forty doors   *24*
   Are built into bright Valhalla:
Eight hundred warriors through one door
   Shall go out to fight with Fenris.

Heath-Run is the goat in the hall of All-Father   *25*
   Who bites at Laerad's boughs:
She shall fill the decanter with clear mead,
   That drink shall never run dry:

Oak-Thorn the hart in the hall of All-Father   *26*
   Who bites at Laerad's boughs:
His horns drip into Hvergelmir,
   Whence all waters rise.

Sid and Vid, Sökin and Eikin,   27
Svöl, Fimbulthul, Fjorm and Gunnthro,
   Rinn and Rennandi,
Gipul and Gopul, Gomul and Geirvimul,
   Encircle the hall of the High Ones,
With Thyn and Vin, Tholl and Holl,
   Grad and Gunnthorin.

Vina is one stream, Vegsvin another,   28
   A third Thjodnuma,
Nyt and Not, Nonn and Hronn,
Slid and Hrid, Sylg and Ylg,
Vid and Van, Vond and Strond,
Gjoll and Leift, they gush down to men
   And afterwards down to Hel.

Thor shall wade through the waters of Ormt,   29
   Kormt and the two Kerlaugs,
When he goes each day to deal out fates
   From Yggdrasil the ash tree.
The bridge of the gods shall burst into flame,
   The sacred waters seethe.

Glad and Gyllir, Gler, Skeidbrimir,   30
   Silfrintop and Sinir,
Gisl, Falhofnir, Gulltop, Lettfeti,
   Are the steeds astride which the gods
Ride each day to deal out fates
   From Yggrdasil the ash tree.

Three roots spread three ways   31
   Under the ash Yggdrasil:
Hel is under the first, Frost Giants under the second,
   Mankind below the last.

Rat-Tusk is the squirrel who shall run up   *32*
    Yggdrasil the ash tree,
Bearing with him the words of the eagle
    Down to Nidhögg beneath.

Four the harts who the high boughs   *33*
    Gnaw with necks thrown back:
Dain and Dvalin, Duneyr and Durathror.

Under Yggdrasil hide more serpents   *34*
    Than dull apes dream of:
Goin and Moin, Grafvitnir's sons,
Sleepbringer, Unraveler, shall bite off
    Twigs of that tree for ever.

The hardships endured by Yggdrasil   *35*
    Are more than men can dream of:
Harts bite the twigs, the trunk rots,
    Nidhögg gnaws at the roots.

My ale-horn is brought me by Hrist and Mist: *36*
    Skegghold and Skogul,
Hildi and Hlokk, Herfjotur, Thrudi,
    Goll and Geirolul,
Rangrid, Radgrid and Reginleif
    Serve ale to the slain,

Up shall rise All-Swift and Early-Awake,   *37*
    Hungry, to haul the Sun:
Under their shoulders shall the gods
    Carry cold iron.

The Cooler he is called who covers the Sun   *38*
    Like a shield, shining for gods:

Fire would consume fell and ocean
   Should his shield fall.

Skoll the wolf who shall scare the Moon   *39*
   Till he flies to the Wood-of-Woe:
Hati the wolf, Hridvitnir's kin,
   Who shall pursue the Sun.

From Ymir's flesh was the earth shaped,   *40*
   From his blood the salt sea,
The fells from his bones, the forests from his hair,
   The arching sky from his skull;
From his eyelashes the High Ones made
   Middle-Earth for men,
And out of his brains the ugly-tempered
   Clouds were all carved.

Ull will grace him, the gods also,   *41*
   Who first reaches the flame:
Open to the gods will all worlds be:
   When the cauldrons are carried off.

The Sons of Invaldi ventured of old   *42*
   To build Skidbladnir,
The best of ships, for bright Frey,
   The nimble son of Njörd.

Of all trees is Yggdrasil best,   *43*
   Skidbladnir best of ships,
Of Gods Odin, of horses Sleipnir,
Bifröst of bridges, Bragi of poets,
Habrok of hawks, and of hounds Garm.

I lift my eyes and look now   *44*
   For aid from all the gods,

All the gods who shall enter to sit
   At the benches in Aegir's Hall.
   And drink in Aegir's Hall.

I am called Grim, I am called Traveler,   *45*
   Warrior and Helmet-Wearer,
Agreable, Third, Thud and Ud,
   High-One and Hel-Blinder.

Truth, Change, and Truth-Getter,   *46*
   Battle-Glad, Abaser,
Death-Worker, Hider, One-Eye, Fire-Eye,
   Lore-Master, Masked, Deceitful.

Broad-Hat, Broad-Beard, Boat-Lord, Rider,   *47*
All-Father, Death-Father, Father of Victory,
But by one name I have never been called
   Since I came among men.

Masked I am called in the courts of Geirrod,   *48*
   But Jalk in Asmund's Hall,
Keeler they say of the sledge-drawer,
   Stirrer-of-Strife at Things,
   Vidur on the field of battle,
Equal-High, Shaker, Shout and Wish,
   Wand-Bearer, Grey-Beard among gods.

Wise and Sage at Sokkmimir's   *49*
   When I hid the old giant:
When I came to Midvitnir's the Killer of the Famed
      One's
   Son sat there alone.

You are drunk, dead drunk, Geirrod,   *50*
Deprived of reason, deprived of my help,
Of the favor of the fallen, of the favor of Odin.

I have told you much, you remember too little,   *51*
    Friends betray your trust:
Already I see the sword of my friend,
    A blade dripping with blood.

Soon shall Ygg have your sword-struck corpse,   *52*
    Your life's race is run:
Hostile are the incubi, Odin can see,
    Draw on me if you dare.

I am now Odin, I was Ygg before,   *53*
    Thud my name before that,
Wakeful and Heavens-Roar, Hanged and Skilfing,
    Goth and Jalk among gods,
Unraveler, Sleep-Bringer: they are really one,
    Many names for me.

Geirrod sat with his sword on his knee, half drawn from its sheath. When he heard that it was Odin, he rose to take him from the fire. The sword slipped and fell hilt down. The king stumbled and fell and the sword pierced him and slew him. Then Odin vanished, but Agnar ruled there as king for a long time.

The Lay of Vafthrudnir

Shall I visit Vafthrudnir?   *1*
   Afford me your counsel, Frigg:
For I long to meet him and match runes
   In a word-joust with the giant.

Father of Warriors, Frigg's counsel   *2*
   Is that you stay at home:
No giant is equal, I judge, in strength
   And thought to Vafthrudnir.

Much have I traveled, much have I learned,   *3*
   Much have I proved the Powers:
I will venture to visit Vafthrudnir
   And see his hall for myself.

   Unharmed go forth, unharmed return,   *4*
      Unharmed back to your own:
   May you, Father of Men, prevail
      In your word-joust with the giant.

   So Odin departed to prove the giant,   *5*
      Match him wit for wit:
   Into the hall of Im's father
      Ygg the Fearsome entered.

   Hail, Friend! From afar I have come   *6*
      To visit you, Vafthrudnir:
   I am eager to learn if you are half-wise
      Or all-wise, as I hear.

Who are you? Who is it dares 7
  To toss at me taunting words?
Unless your lore prove larger than mine,
  You shall not leave here alive.

My name is Gagnrad: now from the road 8
  I enter your hall in need
Of food and drink; far have I traveled
  For your welcome, wise giant.

Tell me, Gagnrad, why you talk from the floor 9
  And do not seat yourself:
You shall prove to me who has more wit,
  The guest or his old host.

A poor man among the wealthy 10
  Must needs speak or be silent:
No good will bragging bring him, I think,
  Who comes to challenge the cunning.

Tell me, Gagnrad — you may talk from the
        floor — 11
  Tell me to test your boldness:
What is the horse called who hauls forth
  Day for the heroic race?

Bright-Mane is he called who the clear day hauls 12
  Forth for the heroic race:
Mightiest is he thought among the Hreidgoths,
  With his golden-gleaming mane.

What is the horse called who from the east drags 13
  Night that seems good to the gods?

Ice-Mane is he called who for all drags   *14*
    Night that seems good to the gods:
Foam from his bit falls each morning,
    Whence comes dew to the dales.

What is the river called that runs between   *15*
    The grounds of giants and gods?

Ifing is the river that runs between   *16*
    The grounds of giants and gods:
Open shall it run for evermore
    And never be iced over.

What is the plain called, the place where Surt   *17*
    Shall finally defeat the gods?

Vigrid is the plain, the place where Surt   *18*
    Shall finally defeat the gods:
A hundred rasts in each direction
    The area is of that plain.

You are wise, guest: go to the bench,   *19*
    Be seated and continue our talk,
To see who in wit is the wiser of us.
    We will stake our heads on the outcome.

Vouch to me first Vafthrudnir,   *20*
    If your wisdom serves you well:
How did the earth, how did the sky,
    Both of them, come to be?

From Ymir's flesh was earth shaped,   *21*
    The mountains from his mighty bones,
From the skull of Frost-Cold was the sky made,
    The salt sea from his blood.

Vouch to me second, Vafthrudnir: 22
Whence comes the moon, whence comes the sun,
    That move alike over men?

Mundilferi is the moon's father   23
    And so of the sun also:
They shall travel through heaven every day
    As a tally of times for men.

Vouch to me third, Vafthrudnir: 24
Whence comes the day, whence comes the night
    And its moons that fare over men?

Delling is the name of Day's father,   25
    But Night was begotten of Nör,
New Moon and Old were made by the gods
    As a tally of times for men.

Vouch to me fourth, Vafthrudnir: 26
Whence came winter and warm summer,
    How did both of them come to be?

Wind-Cold was Winter's father,   27
    South the father of Summer.

Vouch to me fifth, Vafthrudnir: 28
Whence comes the wind that over waves fares,
    Unseen by human eyes?

Hraesvelg sits at the edge of the world,   29
    Huge in eagle feathers:
From his wings, they say, the wind comes
    That fares over mortal men.

Vouch to me sixth, Vafthrudnir: *30*
Who of the gods or of Ymir's kin
  In the First Age was first?

In the endless winters before earth was shaped, *31*
  Then was Bergelmir born:
His father, I think, was Thrudgelmir,
  As Aurgelmir was his.

Vouch to me seventh, Vafthrudnir: *32*
Whence did Aurgelmir come who of all the giants
  In the First Age was first?

From Elivagur venom drops *33*
  Joined to make the giant:
We are all his sons, descended from him,
  Hence we are all so fierce.

Vouch to me eighth, Vafthrudnir *34*
How that grim giant begot children,
  Who never knew a giantess.

Under his armpits the Ice Giant grew *35*
  A boy and a girl together:
Foot by foot the Fierce One begot
  A six-headed son.

Vouch to me ninth, Vafthrudnir, *36*
What you first remember, first knew;
  For you know all, do you not?

In the endless winters before the earth was
      shaped, *37*
  Then was Bergelmir born:

What I first remember is the flour bin
  In which they laid the Wise One.

Vouch to me tenth, Vafthrudnir,   *38*
How Njörd comes to be counted a god,
  To have high altars and temples
Raised to his name though not god-born.

In Vanaheim did the Vanes shape him   *39*
  And gave him as pledge to the gods:
After the Doom of this Age he will return
  Home to the all-wise Vanes.

Vouch to me eleventh, Vafthrudnir: *40*
Who of the men in Odin's court
  Fare to the fight each day?

All the dead warriors in Odin's court   *41*
  Fare to the fight each day:
They select the slain, then leave the battle,
  Sit after at peace in the hall.

Vouch to me twelfth, Vafthrudnir: *42*
From the runes of the giants, from the runes of
      the gods,
  Are you able rightly to read
  What fate shall befall the gods?

From the runes of the giants, from the runes of
      the gods,   *43*
  I can read the truth aright:
  I have wandered through all the worlds;
Through the Nine Worlds and through Nether-Hel
  Where die the heroes from Hel.

Much have I traveled, much have I learned,　　*44*
　　Much have I proved the Powers:
Who will survive when the Arch-Winter
　　Shall kill most of mankind?

In Hoddmimir's Wood shall be hidden from it　*45*
　　Lif and Lifthrasnir:
For meat they shall feed on morning dew,
　　And from both shall men be reborn.

Whence shall come the Sun to the smooth heaven *46*
　　After Fenris has eaten her up?

Elf-Candle shall have a daughter　　*47*
　　Before she is seized by Fenris:
The maid shall ride her mother's highway
　　When all the High Ones are dead.

Who are the maids with minds of wisdom　*48*
　　Who shall glide over the ocean?

Maidens in threes over Mogthrasnir's　　*49*
　　Village wing their way,
Good spirits who guard homes,
　　Although Thurse-begotten.

Who shall inhabit the home of the gods　*50*
　　When Surt's flames slacken?

Vidar and Vali, the virtuous, shall dwell there,　*51*
　　When Surt's flames slacken:
To Modi and Magni shall Mjollnir belong
　　When Thor is overthrown.

By whom in the end shall Odin fall,   52
   When the High Ones are all destroyed?

Fenris will swallow the Father of Men: 53
   This will Vidar avenge,
Cleaving asunder the cold jaws
   In the last fight with Fenris.

What did Odin whisper in the ears of his son   54
   Before Baldur was borne to the pyre?

You alone know that, what long ago   55
   You said in the ears of your son.
I doomed myself when I dared to tell
   What fate will befall the gods,
And staked my wit against the wit of Odin,
   Ever the wisest of all.

The Words of the All-Wise

ALVIS   Put away the benches: for my bride and me   *1*
        It is time to be turning homeward.
    I am eager for this wedding: they are wondering
        there
        Why I linger so long.

THOR   Of what race are you, White-Nose?   2
        Were you clasped in the night by a corpse?
    I think you must be Thurse-begotten:
        You were never born for a bride.

ALVIS   All-Wise I am called: under the ground   *3*
        I dwell in the dark among stones.
    From the Lord of Chariots I look for good faith:
        It is ill to break an oath.

THOR   I never swore one: I was not at home   4
        When the gods gave you this pledge.
    The bride's father has the best right:
        Permission is for me to give.

ALVIS   Declare your name, who claim to be   *5*
        The father of the fair maid.
    Far-wanderer, few know you:
        Whose arm-rings do you wear?

THOR   The lord Ving-Thor, Longbeard's son,   6
        Who has traveled wide in the world:
    Unless I agree, give my consent,
        You shall never marry the maid.

ALVIS You will agree, give your consent   7
          That I shall marry the maid,
       The snow-white woman I desire to have
          Rather than live alone.

THOR   Wise guest, I give you my promise: 8
          I will not deny you her hand,
       If you know what I wish to know concerning
          All the worlds there are.

       Say, Dwarf, for it seems to me   9
          There is nothing you do not know:
       What is earth called, the outstretched land,
          In all the worlds there are?

ALVIS *Earth* by men, *The Fold* by gods,   10
          Vanes call it *The Ways*,
       Giants *Ever-green*, elves *Growing*,
          High gods call it *Clay*.

THOR   What is heaven called, that all know,   11
          In all the worlds there are?

ALVIS *Heaven* by men, *The Arch* by gods,   12
          Wind-Weaver by vanes,
       By giants *High-Earth*, by elves *Fair-Roof*,
          By dwarves *The Dripping Hall*.

THOR   What is the moon called, that men see,   13
          In all the worlds there are?

ALVIS *Moon* by men, *The Ball* by gods,   14
          The Whirling Wheel in Hel,
       The Speeder by giants, *The Bright One* by dwarves,
          By elves *Tally-of-Years*.

THOR   What is sol called, that is seen by men,   *15*
       In all the worlds there are?

ALVIS   *Sol* by men, *Sun* by gods,   *16*
       By dwarves, *Dvalin's Doll*,
    By giants *Everglow*, by elves *Fair-Wheel*,
       All-Bright by sons of gods.

THOR   What are clouds called, that carry rain,   *17*
       In all the worlds there are?

ALVIS   *Clouds* by men, *Hope-of-Showers* by gods,   *18*
       Wind-Ships by vanes,
    By giants *Drizzle-Hope*, by elves *Weather-Might*,
       In Hel *Helmet-of-Darkness*.

THOR   What is wind called, that widely fares   *19*
       In all the worlds there are?

ALVIS   *Wind* by men, *Woe-Father* by gods,   *20*
       By holy powers *The Neigher*,
    The Shouter by giants, *Traveling-Tumult* by elves,
       Squall-Blast they call it in Hel.

THOR   What is calm called, that cannot stir,   *21*
       In all the worlds there are?

ALVIS   *Calm* by men, *Stillness* by gods,   *22*
       Idle-Wind by vanes,
    Over-Warmth by giants, by elves *Day-Quiet*,
       And *Day-Rest* by dwarves.

THOR   What is sea called, that is crossed by men,   *23*
       In all the worlds there are?

ALVIS   *Sea* by men, *Still-Main* by gods,   24
       The vanes call it *Wave*,
   Eel-Home by giants, by elves *Water-Charm*,
       The Dark Deep by dwarves.

THOR   What is fire called, so fierce to men,   25
       In all the worlds there are?

ALVIS   *Fire* by men, *Flame* by gods,   26
       The Flickering One by vanes,
   The Wolfish by giants, *All-Burner* by elves,
       In Hel *The Corpse-Destroyer*.

THOR   What is forest called, that flourishes for men,   27
       In all the worlds there are?

ALVIS   *Forest* by men, *Field's-Mane* by gods,   28
       By heroes *Mountain Sea-Weed*,
   Fire-Wood by giants, *Fair-Bough* by elves,
       By vanes *Wand-of-Charms*.

THOR   What is night called, that Nor fathered,   29
       In all the worlds there are?

ALVIS   *Night* by men, *The Dark* by gods,   30
       By holy powers *The Hood*,
   Unlight by giants, by elves *Sleep-Pleasure*,
       By dwarves *Spinner-of-Dreams*.

THOR   What is the seed called, that is sown by men,   31
       In all the worlds there are?

ALVIS   *Brew* by men, *Barley* by gods,   32
       Vanes call it *The Growth*,

Oats by giants, by elves *Water-Charm*,
 In Hel they call it *The Drooping*.

THOR What is ale called, that is quaffed by men,   *33*
  In all the worlds there are?

ALVIS *Ale* by men, *Beer* by gods,   *34*
  The vanes call it *Strength*,
 Water-Pure by giants, *Mead* in Hel,
  Feast by Sutting's Sons.

THOR Never have I met such a master of lore   *35*
  With such a wealth of wisdom.
 I talked to trick you, and tricked you I have:
  Dawn has broken, Dwarf,
  Stiffen now to stone.

The Lay of Thrym

The Hurler woke, went wild with rage,   *1*
For, suddenly, he missed his sacred Hammer:
He tore his beard, tossed his red locks,
Groped about but could grasp nothing.
Thus, then did Thor speak:
'Loki, Loki, listen well.
Unmarked by men, unmarked by gods,
Someone has stolen my sacred Hammer.'

Fast they went to Freya's quarters.   *2*
Then said Loki, Laufey's Son:
'Freya, will you lend me your feathered cloak
To fly in search of the sacred Hammer?'

'I would give it you gladly, were it gold not feathers, *3*
Part with it now, were it pure silver.'

Then Loki flew — the feathers whistled —   *4*
Out of the door of the Hall of Gods
On and on to the Hall of Giants.
There, on a howe, Thrym sat,
Braiding gold collars for his kennel of hounds,
Unteasing the manes of the mares he loved:
'How fare the gods? How fare the elves?
What brings you on this journey to Gianthome?'

'Ill fare the gods, ill fare the elves.   *5*
Have you taken and hidden the Hammer of
    Thunder?'

'I have taken and hidden the Hammer of Thunder 6
Eight miles deep, way under the ground:
Henceforth no god shall get it back
Till you fetch me Freya for my future bride.'

Then Loki flew — the feathers whistled — 7
Out of the door of the Hall of Giants
On and on to the Hall of Gods.
Meeting him there in the middle court,
Thus then did Thor speak:
'Do you come with a message, not mischief only?
Stand where you are. Let me hear your tidings.
He who sits is seldom truthful,
Who stretches at length a liar always.'

'I come with a message, not mischief only. 8
Thrym stole your Hammer to hide it away.
Henceforth no god shall get it back
Till we fetch him Freya for his future bride.'

Fast they went to Freya's quarters. 9
Then said Loki, Laufey's Son:
'Busk yourself, Freya, in a bridal veil.
You must journey with me to Gianthome.'

Freya snorted with fierce rage, 10
The hall shook and shuddered about them,
Broken to bits was the Brising Necklace:
'In the eyes of the gods a whore I should seem,
If I journeyed with you to Gianthome.'

The gods hastened to their Hall of Judgment, 11
Gathered together, goddesses with them,
Sat in council to consider how
To recover the holy Hammer of Thunder.

Heimdal said, sagest of gods,   *12*
Who could see the future as his fathers did:
'We must busk Thor in a bridal veil,
Hang about him the Brising Necklace,
Bind to his waist a bunch of keys,
Hide his legs in a long dress,
Broad brooches to his breast pin,
With a neat cap cover his locks.'

Thus, then, did Thor speak: *13*
'With coarse laughs you will call me a She
If I busk myself in a bridal veil.'

Loki replied, Laufey's Son: *14*
'Be silent, Thunderer, say no more.
Without the Hammer Asgard is lost.
The giants will dwell here, soon drive us out.'

They busked Thor then in a bridal veil,   *15*
Hung about him the Brising Necklace,
Bound to his waist a bunch of keys,
Hid his legs in a long dress,
Broad brooches to his breast pinned,
With a neat cap covered his locks.

Then said Loki, Laufey's Son: *16*
'I also shall come as your handmaid with you,
We will journey together to Gianthome.'

Quickly the goats were gathered from pasture,   *17*
Hurried into harness: eagerly they ran.
Fire scorched the earth, the fells cracked,
As Thunderer journeyed to Gianthome.

Thus, then did Thrym speak: *18*
'Stand up giants, lay straw on the benches.
They may well bring me my bride now,
Njörd's Daughter, from Noatun.
In my fields there graze gold-horned cattle,
All-black oxen, for my eye's delight.
Much is my treasure, many my gems;
Nothing I lack save lovely Freya.'

Evening came: ale and food   *19*
Were brought to the benches. The bride quickly
Ate a whole ox and eight salmon,
The sweet dainties reserved for the women,
And more than three measures of mead drank.
Thus, then did Thrym speak:
'Was ever bride with appetite so keen,
Ever a bride who took such big mouthfuls,
When was more mead drunk by one maid alone?'

Loki, the handmaid, leaning forward,   *20*
Found the words to befuddle the giant:
'She has not eaten for eight long nights,
So wild her longing for the wedding day.'

Thrym lifted her veil, leaned to kiss her,   *21*
Back he leaped, the full length of the hall:
'How fierce the look in Freya's eyes!
Dangerous the fire that darts out of them.'

Loki, the handmaid, leaning forward,   *22*
Found the words to befuddle the giant:
'She has had no sleep for eight long nights,
So wild her longing for the wedding day.'

The luckless sister of the luckless giant 23
Dared to beg for bridal gifts:
'Give me your rings of red gold,
The rings from your fingers, my favor to win,
My good will, my grace and blessing.'

Thus, then, did Thrym speak: 24
'To bless the bride now bring the Hammer,
Lay Mjöllnir upon the maiden's lap
And wish us joy with joined hands.'

Then in his heart Thunderer laughed, 25
The savage one, when he saw his Hammer.
First Thrym he felled to the ground,
Then all his kin he killed in turn,
Laid low his luckless sister
Who had dared to beg for bridal gifts:
Instead of gold she got a blow,
Instead of rings a rap on the skull.
Thus Thor came to recover his Hammer.

The Lay of Hymir

Long ago the gods had game in abundance,   *1*
Ate their fill, feasting together,
Scored runes and relished blood.
In Aegir's hall there was great plenty.

In the hall sat Fell-Dweller, happy as a child,   *2*
Much like the kin of Miskurblindi,
Till Ygg's son mockingly met his eye:
'Slave, at our feast you shall serve for ever.'

The taunts of the hero troubled the giant,   *3*
His thoughts were turned by them to revenge:
'Let Sif's husband bring in the cauldron
That I may brew ale for all the gods.'

But none of the gods, none of the powers,   *4*
Had such a cauldron; they could not get one.
Until Tyr, the trusty warrior,
Counseled Thunderer with these words.

'Away to the east of Elivagur   *5*
At the sky's end wise Hymir lives,
My savage father: he possesses a kettle,
A magic cauldron, miles deep.'

Then said Thunderer: 'Do you think we can get it?'   *6*
'We can,' said Tyr, 'if cunning enough.'

Long they drove, a day's journey   *7*
From Asgard, till to Egil they came:

They left their goats to graze with him,
And entered the hall where Hymir lived.

Grandson met grandmother: grim she looked,   *8*
A nine-hundred-headed monster:
But white-browed, golden, the wife of Hymir
Brought cups of beer to her son.

'Though you be strong and stout-hearted,   *9*
I had better hide you under the cauldron:
Ungenerous with guests is my giant husband,
And very often ill-tempered.'

Late to his home came the evil-doer,   *10*
Back from the chase; the brutal Hymir
Entered the hall; the icicles clinked
On his chin-forest as the churl came in.

'Now greet, Hymir, with glad mood   *11*
Your son who tonight sits in the hall:
He whom we missed has made his way back.
The comrade with him is called Veur,
Hrod's foe and a friend to man.
Under the gable of the hall they sit,
Protecting themselves with a tall pillar.'

The pillar gave at the glance of the giant,   *12*
The main beam was broken in pieces,
Eight cauldrons, hard-hammered, fell
One by one from the wood shelf:
They stepped out, but the old giant
Held his foe with a fierce gaze.

Hymir was uneasy, beholding before him   *13*
The Peril of Giants pacing his floor:

Then at his orders three bulls
Were led away at once to be boiled.

He made each of them a head shorter,   *14*
They were carried thence to the cooking-fire.
Before sleeping Sif's husband
Ate two oxen all by himself.

Ample indeed Hrungnir's friend   *15*
Thought the repast of Thunderer had been:
'If we three are to eat an evening meal
Of game-meat, we must go hunting.'

Veur said he was ready to row on the waves   *16*
If the villainous giant would provide bait.
'Take your pick of my herd if it pleases you,
Bane of Fell Dwellers, for the bait you need.

There, Veur, I think you will find   *17*
Ox-turds easy to get.'
Quickly the warrior went to the field
Where, all-black, an ox was grazing.

The Bane of Giants broke off   *18*
Its two horns from the high place.
'Much worse do I deem your deeds now,
Keel Wielder, than when you were sitting.'

The Goat Lord bade the Brother of Apes   *19*
To steer the ship a stretch further,
But the giant was weary, weak already,
And little eager for a longer row.

Fierce Hymir on his fish hook   *20*
Drew up two whales at one cast:

Aft in the stern, Odin's son,
Veur, with patience prepared his line.

With an ox-head his angle he baited,   *21*
The slayer of serpents, the savior of men:
From his hook gaped the gods' foe,
Who under the seas encircles the world.

Doughty Thor drew boldly   22
The hideous serpent up on board,
Struck with his hammer the high hair-mountain
Of the writhing Coiler, Kin of the Wolf.

The monster roared, the mountains echoed,   *23*
Middle Earth was mightily shaken
Then the serpent-fish sank back.

Rueful was the giant as they rowed back,   *24*
Far too angry and afraid to speak,
As he labored to catch a lee wind.

'Now you will have to do half the work,   *25*
If I am to get home with my whales
And our sea-buck bring to harbor.'

Sif's husband seized the stern   *26*
Of the sea-stallion, swung it up
With its bilge water, oars and bailing-can,
And bore the giant's brim-swine home
Past the boiling springs and the birch-scrub.

Hymir, though, would not own he was beaten,   *27*
But continued still to contend with Thor:
'Stoutly you row, but strong you are not
Unless you can break this beaker of mine.'

Thunderer took it and threw it quickly   *28*
At a stone column that cracked in pieces
And fell down, but the drinking cup,
When they brought it to Hymir, was undamaged.

Then whispered the beautiful wife of the giant *29*
A secret known to herself alone:
'Harder than the cup is Hymir's skull;
If you want to smash it, smite him there.'

The Lord of Goats got to his feet,   *30*
Exerted every ounce of his strength:
Whole remained Hymir's helmet-stump,
But the wine cup was cracked in half.

Seeing the shattered shards on his knees, *31*
The giant lamented: 'Many good things
Are gone from me, I know; I may never say
From now on — "Ale, be brewed!"

It is yet to be proved that you can bear *32*
Out of this hall my ale-kettle.'
Tyr tried twice to budge it,
But still the cauldron stood where it was.

Sif's husband seized the rim,   *33*
His feet broke through the floor of the hall:
He lifted to his head the huge cauldron;
The pot-rings clashed and clattered at his heels.

They had not gone far before he looked *34*
Round behind him: Odin's son
Saw, then, coming from caves in the east,
Hymir with a many-headed throng.

He lifted the kettle, loosed it from his shoulders,   *35*
And swung Mjöllnir: he slew all
Those wilderness monsters with his murderous
       hammer.

They had not gone far before he observed   *36*
That Thunderer's goat had gone lame:
The Puller on the Harness was half dead.
That was malicious Loki's doing.

But you have all heard, all who are skilled   *37*
In the lore of the gods, what later happened,
How the waste-dweller was rewarded in return:
Both his sons were the price he paid for that.

The Strong One came to the Council of gods,   *38*
Entered with the cauldron Hymir had possessed,
And all the gods from now on could drink
Ale at Aegir's every winter.

The Lay of Erik

ODIN   Before dawn in a dream I saw   *1*
Valhalla preparing to honor the dead;
Busy at my bidding was the band of warriors,
Benches they strewed and beer jugs washed,
And the Valkyrie brought out the best wine.
I expect men from Middle Earth,
Great warriors such as gladden my heart.

Bragi, it thunders like a thousand fighters,   *2*
    A mighty host is on the march.

BRAGI   The benches tremble as though Baldur were
          coming   *3*
    Back to Odin's hall.

ODIN   Foolish are your words, wise Bragi,   *4*
    Erik it is, as you know,
For whom all echoes: he will enter soon,
    The boar, into Odin's Hall.

Sigmund! Sinfjotli! swiftly now   *5*
    Go to greet the prince
And bid him welcome, if he be Erik,
    The hero I am expecting.

BRAGI   Why Erik rather than other princes?   *6*

ODIN   In many lands he has marched to battle   *7*
    And borne a bloody sword.

BRAGI   Why rob of victory so valiant a man?   *8*

ODIN   Who knows what awaits us? Even now he peers,   *9*
     The Gray Wolf, into the gods' dwelling.

    Hail, Erik! Valhalla greets you.   *10*
     You are welcome, wise one, here.
    Tell me, I ask, what troop follows you,
     Boars from the clash of blades?

ERIK   Famous are they all, five kings: *11*
     I am the sixth myself.

The Treachery of Asmund

INNSTEIN   Let us go landgates, leaving the ships,   *1*
All our host, all the spearmen,
To burn Asmund's Hall with fire,
Fall on his troops and take their lives.

HALF   We should send, rather, a small band   *2*
To march from the sea and make peace:
Asmund has offered in earnest of friendship
Many rings of red gold.

INNSTEIN   Small insight have you into Asmund's mind;   *3*
The king is cunning, cruel in heart:
I counsel you, Prince, to put little
Store of trust in your stepfather.

HALF   Asmund has pledged his promise to us   *4*
With solemn oaths as are sworn among men:
A good king will not go against his word,
Will never betray another warrior.

INNSTEIN   Odin, Half, must be angry with you: *5*
Unwise your faith in the word of the king.
Asmund, I tell you, will betray us unless
We guard ourselves against his wiles.

HALF   It pleases you well to prophesy ill.   *6*
The king will surely keep the peace:
Goodwill and welcome await us in his court,
Rings of gold and rich jewels.

INNSTEIN   A dream came to me — dwell on it, Half!   7
Fierce flames flickered about us;
To break loose was no light work.
What meaning, Prince, do you make of my
    dream?

HALF   That I shall give a gleaming helmet   8
To each bold fighter who follows me;
Helmets will blaze like bright fire
On the hair-hills of the host of Skoldings.

INNSTEIN   My second dream — consider it, Half!   9
My shoulders were scorched, shrivelled by
    flames;
Ill, not good, my heart forebodes.
What meaning, Prince, do you make of my
    dream?

HALF   That bright on the backs of battle-wise
    warriors,   10
Shining on the shoulders of the shield-bearers,
Of each bold fighter who follows me,
Golden byrnies shall blaze like fire.

INNSTEIN   My third dream — think on it, Half!   11
We all lay dead in the depths of the sea,
Betrayed by the wiles of the troll-like chief.
What meaning, Prince, do you make of my
    dream?

HALF   Enough! I have listened too long to your
    fears.   12
I command you, Innstein, to hold your peace
And speak no more in my hearing
From henceforth of your foolish dreams.

INNSTEIN   Hearken to me, men of Rogaland,   *13*
Hearken, Hrok, and Utstein too;
Let the host now landgates march,
Nor trust, like Half, in Asmund's word.

UTSTEIN   Let us, rather, allow our Prince   *14*
To say what shall be, decide our journey:
Let us follow him; if our fearless leader
So rule, we will risk our lives.

INNSTEIN   Of old my Prince took pleasure in my counsel, *15*
Many times we marched forward,
But since we landed on this luckless shore,
My words are not spoken to a will to hear.

They went to Asmund's Hall, feasted and fell asleep. When they woke, the hall was filled with smoke. They armed themselves and prepared for battle. Innstein said:

INNSTEIN   There is smoke above the hawks in the Hall of
        the King;   *16*
Wax from our sword-points soon will drip.
It is time for the gold, the twinkling gems,
And the helmets to be offered to Half's warriors.

Awake, Half! All about us   *17*
Your grim-minded kin have kindled fires;
Jewels of flame are the gems they offer,
Pleasing presents you must pay back.

Finish, friends, the foaming ale,   *18*
The stout pillars are starting to crack.
Men shall remember while men live
The march of our host to the maker of war.

Go boldly forward nor fall back: 19
Our foes shall learn to fear our sword-play;
Cruel scars they shall carry hence,
Bloody limbs before the battle ends.

Brave youths, break through the wall   20
Of glowing fire with our gallant Prince;
No man is allowed to live forever:
The furnisher of rings will not flinch at death.

They broke out of the hall, but Half fell among his men.
Innstein said:

INNSTEIN I have watched them all, as one following,   21
Equal in courage, the king's son;
We shall meet again when we go hence;
Life is a burden no lighter than death.

Hrok has fallen at the feet of his Prince,   22
The young warrior, wolf-bold:
It is ill to yield up to All-Father,
Robbed of victory, so valiant a man.

For eighteen summers I have set forth,   23
Ridden with the host to redden our spears:
Never shall I know another lord
Nor gladness in battle, nor grow old.

Stretched on the earth shall Innstein lie,   24
Here by the head of Half, his Prince:
Men shall remember while men live
That the Lord of Rogaland laughed as he died.

The Waking of Angantyr

| | A young maiden met at sunset | *1* |
| | A man with his flock on Munarvag. | |

| HERDSMAN | To visit this island all alone | *2* |
| | Is overbold: go back to your lodging. | |

HERVOR	I have no lodging: of the island folk	*3*
	I know none. I will not go back.	
	Before we part, first tell me	
	How I may come to the Hjorvard graves.	

HERDSMAN	Do not ask: it is unwise.	*4*
	You do not know your deadly peril:	
	Let us flee as fast as our feet can take us,	
	All without is a horror to view.	

HERVOR	It is vain to hinder the viking's friend.	*5*
	Show me the way: as a reward you shall have	
	This gold necklace: you will get nothing,	
	Nor ring nor ornament if you hold your peace.	

HERDSMAN	To have come hither, all alone	*6*
	To this land of shadows, was sheer folly.	
	Over fen and fold fires are soaring,	
	Graves are opening: let us go quickly.	

HERVOR	Fear not the fire, fear not the graves:	*7*
	Although the island be all aflame,	
	Never shall warriors while they live	
	Yield to terror. Tell me the way.	

The herdsman had taken to his heels
    already,   *8*
Fled to the wood, far from the maiden,
But the fierce heart in Hervor's breast
Swelled up at the sight of these things.

*She saw now the grave-fires and the graves standing open.
She went to the howe and was not afraid. She passed the fires
as if they were smoke, until she reached the graves of the
berserks. Then she said:*

HERVOR   Angantyr, wake! Hervor calls you,   *9*
                  Your only daughter whom you had by Tofa.
                  Give up from the grave the gleaming sword
                  That the dwarves smithied for Svafrlami.

                  Hervard, Hjorvard, Hrani, awake!   *10*
                  Hear me, all of you, under the tree-roots,
                  With sharp swords, with shields and byrnies
                  And red spears, the rig of war.

                  Much are you changed, children of
                      Arngrim,   *11*
                  Once so mighty: are you mold now?
                  Will Eyfura's sons refuse to listen
                  Or speak with me on Munarvag?

                  May ants shred you all to pieces,   *12*
                  Dogs rend you; may you rot away.
                  Give back the sword that was smithied by
                      Dvalin:
                  Fine weapons are unfit for ghosts.

ANGANTYR   Evil it is, Hervor, my daughter,   *13*
                  To call down such curses upon us:

Your words are mad, without meaning in
    them.
Why do you wake the bewildered dead?

Nor father nor brothers buried me deep.   *14*
Tyrfing was owned by two who live,
Though only one owned it later.

HERVOR   Tell me the truth, that the timeless gods   *15*
May bless your grave. Have you got Tyrfing?
Why are you unwilling to yield
Your heritage to your only child?

*Then it was as if a flame lit up all the graves which stood
open. Then Angantyr said:*

ANGANTYR   Graves open and Hel's doors,   *16*
The island surface is one searing flame,
All without is a horror to view:
Go, while there's time: return to your ship.

HERVOR   With no flames, tonight or ever,   *17*
With no fire can you frighten me,
Nor daunt the heart in your daughter's breast
With ghosts standing at grave-mouths.

ANGANTYR   Hear me, Hervor, hear from me now,   *18*
Daughter of princes, the doom I fortell:
This Tyrfing will, if the true blade,
Destroy your kindred, kill them all.

You will bear a son, a bold warrior,   *19*
Who shall wield Tyrfing, trust in its strength:
After Heidrick shall the hero be named,
The bravest one under heaven.

103

HERVOR   Churlish cowards! may my curse fall   *20*
On all of you: may you ever lie
Wretched shades, in the rot of the pit.
Give back the wondrous work of smiths:
Son of Vikings, it is vain to hide it.

ANGANTYR   No mortal maiden to me you seem,   *21*
Who walk in the dark where the dead lie,
Uncowed by flames, with a carved spear
And mailed corselet on Munarvag.

HERVOR   A mortal maiden to men I seemed   *22*
Until advised to visit your halls:
Surrender the blade, the Bane-of-Shields,
Hater-of-Byrnies, Hjalmar's-Killer.

ANGANTYR   Hjalmar's-Killer lies under my shoulders,   *23*
The sharp sword, sheathed in flame:
No maiden on earth, no mortal dare
Touch such a weapon, take it to hold.

HERVOR   I will touch the weapon, take hold of   *24*
The sharp edge. In order to get it
I will walk through fire with unflinching
       step:
The flames are sinking before my eyes.

ANGANTYR   Reckless maiden, rather than see you   *25*
Fling yourself on the flames and perish,
I will grant what you ask, give you the blade:
Such courage of heart I cannot refuse.

HERVOR   You have done well, dead warrior,   *26*
To grant what I ask, give me the blade:

To possess the sword seems to me better
Than to own all Norway.

ANGANTYR   Alas, daughter, little you know,   *27*
Wretched woman, at what you rejoice:
I tell you again, this Tyrfing will
Destroy your kindred, kill them all.

HERVOR   With a glad heart I will go now   *28*
To ride the horses of the roaring sea:
Little care I what may come after,
What dole my sons may deal each other.

ANGANTYR   Long may you hold it and long enjoy it!   *29*
But conceal it well. Beware the edges
Of Hjalmar's-Bane: both are poisoned.
Mortal to man is the Measurer-of-Fate.

Farewell, daughter: would I could give you *30*
All the strength and stoutness of heart
That was taken from Arngrim's twelve sons,
The good of life they lost in death.

HERVOR   I will hasten hence: I am eager to be gone. *31*
Blessed in your graves, may you be at peace.
I deemed in my mind that death was near
When all about me leaped high flame.

The Lay of Völund

Three maidens through Mirkwood flew,   1
Fair and young, fate to endure:
Winged maidens by the water's edge
Peacefully retted precious flax.

Ölrun was the first; she took Egil for lover.   2
Swanwhite the second: she took Slagfidur.
Hervor the third; she threw round Völund's
White neck wanton arms.

So they sat for seven winters,   3
Then in the eighth for home they longed,
In the ninth their dooms drove them apart:
Three maidens through Mirkwood flew,
Fair and young, fate to endure.

The weather-wise hunters, Egil, Slagfidur,   4
Returned from the hunt. The hall was silent:
They searched all about but could see no one.

East after Ölrun Egil rode,   5
South after Swanwhite Slagfidur,
But Völund sat in Wolfdale alone.

Red rings he forged, enriched them with jewels,   6
Rings he threaded upon ropes of bast,
Faithfully waiting for the fair-haired
Hervor to return to his hearth-side.

When the Lord of the Njars, Nidud, heard   7
That Völund sat in Wolfdale alone,

He sent warriors forth: white their shield-bosses
In the waning moon, and their mail glittered.

They drew rein when they got to the gabled hall, *8*
In they came through the end door,
Rings they saw, on ropes threaded:
Seven hundred, all owned by Völund.

These they unthreaded, but there they left them, *9*
All but one, just one they took.
Then the weather-wise hunter, Völund, came
On light feet back from a long road.

He piled up logs, prepared for roasting *10*
A brown bear: well burned the fire
Of wind-dried wood before Völund's eyes.

The lord of the elves lay on a bearskin, *11*
Counting his rings; a red one he missed:
He deemed in his mind that the daughter of Hlovde,
Hervor, had returned to his hearthside.

Long he sat till asleep he fell; *12*
What he knew when he woke was not joy:
He saw on his hands heavy chains,
His feet in fetters were fast bound.

'Who are the men who my hands have chained? *13*
Who have fettered my feet together?'

Then the lord of the Njars, Nidud, answered: *14*
'What good have you gotten, greatest of elves,
From our treasure, Völund, in Wolfdale?'

Then said Völund:

'Was there not gold on Grani's Road?   15
Far thought I our realm from the Rhine hills.
Greater treasure we had in olden days,
At home in the hall, happy together,
Hladgud and Hervor, Hlovde's children,
And wise-counselling Ölrun, Kjar's daughter.'

*Nidud the king gave his daughter, Bodvild, the gold ring he
had taken from the bast at Völund's. And he himself wore the
sword which had been Völund's.*

Without stood the wily one, wife of Nidud,   16
In she came through the end door,
Stood there smiling and softly whispered:
'Woeful shall be he who from the wood comes.'

He gnashes his teeth when he notices the sword,   17
And on Bodvild's arm beholds his ring,
His eyes glare, grim as a snake's:
With a knife they cut his knee-sinews,
Set him on the island of Saeverstod.

*There he fashioned all sorts of precious things for the king.
And no man except the king dared to voyage thither.*

'From Nidud's hip there hangs a sword,   18
The blade I sharpened with a sure eye,
The blade I tempered with a true hand;
Now the shining steel is stolen from me:
Back to my smithy it shall be born yet.'

'Bitterest to bear, bitterest to behold,   19
Bodvild wearing my wife's ring.'

Fierce, unsleeping, at his forge he hammered,   *20*
Making for Nidud marvelous things:
He saw two boys, the sons of Nidud,
At the door of his smithy on Saeverstod.

They beheld a chest, they asked for a key.   *21*
Evil was on them as in they looked.
There were gems in plenty, precious stones,
And red gold to gladden their eyes.

'Come tomorrow, but come alone,   *22*
Gold and gems I will give you both.
Tell not the maidens, tell not the courtiers,
Let no one know of our next meeting.'

So they returned, the two brothers,   *23*
Said to each other: 'Let us see the rings.'
They beheld a chest, they asked for a key.
Evil was on them as in they looked.

He struck off the heads of those stalwart boys,   *24*
Under soot-blackened bellows their bodies hid,
From both their skulls he scraped the hair
And set them in silver as a sight for Nidud,
Of their eyes he fashioned excellent gems
For his dear neighbor, Nidud's wife,
And out of the teeth which were in their mouths
He forged a brooch to bring Bodvild joy.

Precious beyond all price to Bodvild   *25*
Was the ring she had broken; she brought it to Völund:
'None but you are to know of this.'

'Mend it I can so the marred gold   *26*
Shall appear to your father fairer still,

109

In your mother's eyes look much much better,
While to you it will seem the same as before.'

Ale he brought her, the artful smith: 27
Long they sat till asleep she fell.
'Now all but one for my hurts are paid,
All but the most evil of women.'

'I wish that my knees be well again,   28
My limbs that were maimed by the men of
    Nidud.'
Laughing rose Völund, aloft in the air,
Weeping fled Bodvild, away from the isle,
Afraid of her lover and her father's wrath.

Without stood the wily one, wife of Nidud,   29
In she came through the end door.
The lord of the Njars lay there resting:
'Nidud, husband, are you awake?'

'Awake am I ever and without joy,   30
Little I sleep since my sons are gone,
Cold is my head, cold were your whisperings,
Now with Völund I wish to speak.

'Learn me, Völund, lord of the elves: 31
Where are my boys? What has befallen them?'

'Oaths first shall you all swear me,   32
By ship's-keel, by shield's rim,
By stallion's-shoulder, by steel's-edge,
That you will not harm the wife of Völund

Nor cause the death of his dear bride,
Who shall in the hall bring up our child.

'Go to my forge which your folly built,   *33*
There find the bellows blood-bespattered.
I struck off the heads of your stalwart boys,
Under soot-blackened bellows their bodies hid,

'From both their skulls I scraped the hair   *34*
And set them in silver as a sight for Nidud,
Of their eyes I fashioned excellent gems
For my dear neighbor, Nidud's wife,

'And out of the teeth which were in their mouths   *35*
I forged a brooch to bring Bodvild joy,
Bodvild who goes now great with child,
Your only daughter, dear to you both.'

'Never have words brought woe more bitter.   *36*
For vengeance, Völund, in vain must I long.
No man is so tall to take you from your horse,
No sharp-eyed archer can shoot you down,
There where you hang, high in the clouds.'

Laughing, Völund rose aloft in the air: *37*
Sorrowing, Nidud sat there after.

'Thakrad, best of thralls, go quickly,   *38*
Go to Bodvild, the bright-browed maiden,
Bid her come forth; her father awaits her.

'Is it true, Bodvild, as I am told it is,   *39*
That you and Völund, when you visited him
On the lone island, lay together?'

'It is true, Nidud, as you were told it was.   *40*
Völund and I, when I visited him
On the lone island, lay together.
A day of ill-omen, an hour of sin.
Against his wiles I had no wit to struggle,
Against his will I did not want to struggle.'

Brunhild's Hel-Ride

After the death of Brunhild, two pyres were laid: one for Sigurd, which was ignited first; on the other, Brunhild was burnt, atop a hearse covered with a rich cloth. It is told how Brunhild rode the hearse down the Hel-way, and passed the house of a giantess. The giantess said:

'Depart! You shall not pass through   *1*
My tall gates of towering stone:
It befits a wife to wind yarn,
Not to know another's husband.

'To what end, woman from Gaul,   *2*
False of heart, would you enter my realm?
Fair woman, if you want the truth,
You have bathed your hands in the blood of men.'

'Bar me not, bride of stone-elves!   *3*
They think me the higher, those who know
Both our births, better than you.'

'You were born, Brunhild, Budli's daughter,   *4*
Of all women the worst fated,
Brought sorrow and death to the Sons of Gjuki,
Down to nothing their noble house.'

'I shall tell you, giantess, joyless news,   *5*
News of the worst, if you want the truth:
Gjuki's Sons by guile made me
A loveless bride, a breaker of oaths.

113

'Hild-under-helm they all called me,   6
All who knew me in Hlymdale,
Where, under the oak, over eight sisters
Valfather flung feathered cloaks.
Twelve winters I knew, if you want the truth,
When I plighted my troth to the peerless warrior.

'Hjalm-Gunnar to Hel I sent,   7
The old Goth, when I gave victory
To young Agnar, Autha's Brother:
Angry with me was Odin for that.

'He scarfed me in shields on Skatalund,   8
Red and white ones, their rims interlocked,
With a sleep-spell bound me, and bade Tree-Foe
Burn all about the bed where I lay.

'Then the hero, the thane who never   9
Had felt fear, through the flames rode
To fetch thence Fafnir's Hoard
And rouse me at last from my long sleep.

'On Grani he rode, the gold-sharer,   10
To the Hall where my foster-father ruled:
In the King's host, he was counted best,
Viking of the Danes, most valiant of all.

'In a single bed we slept and were happy: 11
As if we had been brother and sister,
Neither laid a lustful hand
Upon the other for eight nights.

'Then Gjuki's daughter, Gudrun, mocked me,   12
Said I had slept in Sigurd's arms:

114

I found then, what I fain would have not,
That through a trick I had taken a husband.

'Men and women on Middle Earth   *13*
Must contend with grief and for too long:
Never shall Sigurd be sundered from me;
None shall unjoin us. Giantess, yield!'

Baldur's Dreams

The gods hurried to their Hall of Council,   *1*
Gathered together, goddesses with them,
All-powerful, eager to unriddle
Baldur's dream that such dread portended.

Up rose Odin, unaging magician,   *2*
Harnessed Sleipnir, the eight-legged,
Sped down fron Heaven to Hel's Deep.
The blood-dabbled Hound of Hel faced him,
Howling in frenzy at the Father of Runes.
The High One halted at the eastern gate,
Where loomed a tumulus, tomb of a witch.
Runes he chanted, charms of power:
Her spectre rose whom his spell commanded
To enlighten the god with the lore of the dead.

'Who is he that on Hel intrudes?   *3*
Who calls me up, increasing my grief?
Drenched by hail, driven by storm,
Dew-frozen, I am dead long.'

'I am Struggler's Son, Strider, Way-Tamer,   *4*
Your secrets I ask: all earth's I know.
Why are Hel's halls hung with jewels,
Her chambers rivers of red gold?'

'For Baldur our mead is brewed strong   *5*
In a shining cauldron, a shield over it.
Odin on high in heart despairs.
Unwilling my words: I would no more.'

'Far-seeing witch, your words unriddle.   6
More will I ask: all will I know.
Who shall slay Baldur, best of the gods,
Who suck the life from the Son of Odin?'

'Hödur the Blind the branch shall throw,   7
From his brother's body the blood to drain,
Sucking the life from the Son of Odin.
Unwilling my words: I would no more.'

'Far-seeing witch, your words unriddle.   8
More will I ask: all will I know.
By whose hand shall Hödur fall
And Baldur's Bane be burned with fire?'

'Rindur the Blessed shall bring forth Vali.   9
Though but a night old, he shall be the avenger,
His hands he shall wash not nor his hair comb
Till Baldur's Bane is borne to the pyre:
Unwilling my words: I would no more.'

'Far-seeing witch, your words unriddle.   10
More will I ask: all will I know.
Who are the maidens who shall mourn then,
Toss up to heaven their trailing scarves?'

'Way-Tamer you are not, nor are you Strider: 11
You are Odin the Wily, unaging magician.'

'Witch you are not, nor woman either: 12
Womb of monsters, you have mothered three.'

'Go home, Odin: air your triumph.   13
No guest shall again my grave visit,
Till wild Loki tear loose from his bonds
And the World-Wasters on the warpath come.'

117

Skirnir's Ride

SKADI	Arise, Skirnir, ride now	*1*
	Swiftly to Frey, my son,	
	And ask him this: with whom is the wise one	
	So angry, so sad at heart?	

SKIRNIR   A grim answer I shall get, Skadi,   *2*
       I fear, from Frey, your son,
If I ask him this: at whom is the wise one
       So angry, so sad at heart?

           Tell me, Frey, first of the gods,   *3*
       That which I long to learn:
Why do you sit and sulk in your hall
       Alone, my lord, all day?

FREY   Why should I tell you what is the cause   *4*
       Of the great grief that casts
Gloom on my mind, though the Glory of Elves
       Lights up the daytime hours.

SKIRNIR   No grief, Prince, is so great that you   *5*
       May not tell it to me:
In the days of our youth we were young
          together,
       Each can trust the other.

FREY   I saw a girl in Gymir's courts,   *6*
       A girl for whose love I long:
Air and water took on a radiance
       From the light of her lovely arms.

As dear to no man in days past   7
   Was maid as she is to me:
But no elf, no god, will grant my prayer
   That I may lie with her.

SKIRNIR   Give me a mare that will gallop through   8
   The wall of flickering flame,
And the sword that slays by itself when battle
   Is joined with the race of giants.

FREY   I will give you a mare that will gallop
       through   9
   The wall of flickering flame,
And the sword that slays by itself if brave
   The warrior be who wields it.

SKIRNIR   Night has fallen: now we must ride   10
   Over the misty mountains,
The fells of the troll-folk;
We shall both arrive or both fall into
   The hands of the horrible giant.

Hail, herdsman, howe-watcher,   11
   Looking this way and that!
By what means can I speak, despite his
       hounds,
   With Gymir's daughter, Gerd.

HERDSMAN   Are you doomed to death, or dead already?   12
Barred shall you ever be from speech
   With Gymir's daughter, Gerd.

SKIRNIR   To stake life on the luck of the dice   13
   Is better than to be a coward:

119

The day of my death is destined already,
    By Fate my time is fixed.

GERD   What is the noise which now I hear,   *14*
    That din throughout our halls?
Earth trembles, everything shakes
    In the wide garths of Gymir.

HERDSMAN   A man on a mare: he dismounts and leads
            her   *15*
    Unbridled to graze the grass.

GERD   Go, let him in; bid him enter our hall   *16*
    And drink a draught of mead,
Though my heart forebodes that my brother's
            killer
    Darkens the door with his shadow.

Are you one of the elves, are you one of the
            gods,   *17*
    Or one of the wise Vanes?
Why have you ridden through wildfire
    Hither to visit our halls?

SKIRNIR   I am not an elf, I am not a god,   *18*
    Nor one of the wise Vanes,
Though well I have ridden through wildfire
    Hither to visit your halls.

Eleven apples, all of gold,   *19*
    Lo, I will give them you, Gerd,
To look on Frey with friendly eyes,
    Call him your dearest dear.

GERD No, your apples I will never take *20*
  At any wooer's wish,
Nor look on Frey with friendly eyes,
  Nor call him my dearest dear.

SKIRNIR This bracelet I'll give you, that was burned
    on the pyre *21*
  Of Baldur, Odin's boy:
It drops eight of equal thickness
  Every ninth night.

GERD I refuse the bracelet, though burned on the
    pyre *22*
  Of Baldur, Odin's boy:
I need no gold in Gymir's court;
  His wealth is at my command.

SKIRNIR Do you see this sword, slender, inwrought, *23*
  This sword I hold in my hand?
I will hack your head from your haughty neck
  Unless you pledge your love.

GERD No threat of force shall frighten me *24*
  To yield to a wooer's wish:
If Gymir, my father, finds you here,
  Short shrift you will get.

SKIRNIR Do you see this sword, slender, inwrought, *25*
  This sword I hold in my hand?
Beneath its edge will the old one kneel,
  It dooms your father to die.

With a taming wand I shall teach you
    swiftly, *26*
  Make you, maiden, obey.

You shall be sent where no son of man
    Or god shall see you again,
With earth behind you, on an eagle's mound,
    Facing Hel, for ever sit.
Fouler to you shall food look
    Than the snake seems to warriors.
A sight you shall become ere you come out.
Hrimnir shall leer at you, everyone jeer at you,
    A more famous figure you'll be
Than the god's watchman when you gape
        through the fence.
May error and terror, blotches and blains,
    Grow on you, grief with tears.
Crouch low while the curse I pronounce,
Heavy torment and twofold grief.
Orcs shall pinch you the whole day long
    In the grim garths of the giants,
Every day to the halls of Frost
    You shall creep, crawl without choice,
    Without any hope of choice
Lamentation not laughter know,
    Dejection instead of joy.
With three-headed trolls shall your time be
        spent,
    Never shall a man come near you,
May your senses be numbed, your sadness
        weep,
May you be as the thistle, thoughtlessly
        crushed
    Underfoot at the gate of the garth.
To the woods I went, through the wet trees,
    For a spell-binding branch,
    And a fitting branch I found.
Odin is angry, angry is Thor,

All the gods shall hate you;
Base maiden, you have brought on yourself
   The anger of all the gods.
Hear me, giants, hear me frost-trolls,
   Sons of Suttung, hear me,
What I forebode, what I forbid,
   Joy of man to this maid,
   Love of man to this maid.
Hrimgrimir shall have you, the hideous troll,
   Beside the doors of the dead,
Under the tree-roots ugly scullions
   Pour you the piss of goats;
Nothing else shall you ever drink,
   Never what you wish,
   Ever what I wish.
I score troll-runes, then I score three letters,
   Filth, frenzy, lust:
I can score them off as I score them on,
   If I find sufficient cause.

GERD   You have conquered, warrior. This cup I
            pledge you,   27
       Full of foaming mead,
    Little did I dream my love would ever
       Be vowed to a son of the Vanes.

SKIRNIR   More must I know for the message I bear   28
       When I ride from Gymir's garth.
    Where will you meet, when will you give
       Yourself to the Son of Njörd?

GERD   In the woods of Barri which we both know,   29
       A peaceful, secluded place,
    After nine nights to Njörd's Son
       Gerd will give herself.

FREY   Answer me, Skirnir, ere you dismount *30*
      Or step a foot further:
     Is it joyful news from Gianthome
      You bring with you or bad?

SKIRNIR In the woods of Barri which we both know, *31*
      A peaceful, secluded place,
     After nine nights to Njörd's Son
      Gerd will give herself.

FREY   Long is one night, longer are two,   *32*
      Endless the thought of three.
     Many a month has moved more swiftly
      Than this half of a bridal eve.

The Lay of Harbard

Thor was returning from a journey to the east and came to a sound; on the other side of the sound was the ferryman with a boat. Thor cried out:

THOR   Who is that fool of fools on the far shore?   *1*

HARBARD   Who is that clown of clowns who calls across the
             fjord?   2

THOR   Ferry me over: I will feed you this morning.   *3*
         In the bag on my back are the best of foods,
         Herrings and goatmeat: I am glutted with
             them.
         Before I left home I ate my fill.

HARBARD   You would never praise them if you knew all: *4*
         Your kin are mourning: your mother is dead.

THOR   What you say is the saddest thing   *5*
         A man can hear — that my mother is dead.

HARBARD   You don't look like a lord with lands of your
             own: 6
         Without breeches, barefooted,
           You look more like a tramp.

THOR   Row over your boat and beach it where I
             show you.   7
         Who owns the boat you hold to the shore?

HARBARD	Battle-Wolf: he is wise in counsel	8
	And sits in a hall on the sound of Radsey.	
	I am ordered to refuse horse-thieves and robbers,	
	Accept only those I can see are honest:	
	Tell me your name if you would travel across.	

THOR   I would tell you my name, tell you my
                      lineage,   9
                Were I an outlaw: I am Odin's son,
                Meili's brother and Magni's father,
                The god who throws. With Thor you deal.
                In turn I bid you tell me your name.

HARBARD   My name is Harbard: I hide it seldom.   10

THOR   Why hide your name if not condemned?   11

HARBARD   Though condemned, unless I be doomed to
                      fall,   12
                I would save my life from such as you.

THOR   Demeaning it would be to wade over   13
                And ruin my gear: you will get what you
                      deserve
                For your clodhopper's taunts if I cross the fjord.

HARBARD   Wade away: I will wait for you.   14
                No harder man have you met since Hrungnir
                      died.

THOR   How dare you refer to my fight with
                      Hrungnir,   15
                The stout-hearted giant with a stone head!

I struck him down; he fell dead before me.
   Meanwhile, what were you doing?

HARBARD   I was with Fjolver for five winters.   *16*
We fought battles, felled heroes,
And wooed maidens: we had much to do.

THOR   How were the women you won there?   *17*

HARBARD   Lively they were, once they were tamed,   *18*
Wise too, once they grew faithful:
Out of sea-sand they spun ropes,
Dug out the bottoms of deep valleys.
Among those fair ones I was first in counsel:
   With seven sisters I dallied
   And had my way with them all.
   Meanwhile, what were you doing?

THOR   The mighty-thewed Thjazi I slew,   *19*
Cast the eyes of the son of All-Wielder
   Up into bright heaven:
They are the mightiest marks of my works,
Hereafter to be seen by all mankind.
   Meanwhile, what were you doing?

HARBARD   With potent love-charms I lured from their
       husbands   *20*
   Hateful night-riding hags:
A hard giant I thought Hlebard to be;
   He brought me a magic branch,
   But I charmed away his wits.

THOR   For his good gifts you gave him evil.   *21*

HARBARD One oak gets the fruit that falls from
                another: 22
      It is each for himself at all times.
      Meanwhile, what were you doing?

THOR I was in the east, the home of the giants, 23
    And thrashed their brides on their way back
        to the fells:
    The giants would rule all, if all were alive,
    All men lie dead under Middle Earth.
      Meanwhile, what were you doing?

HARBARD I was in Gaul: I egged on to battle 24
    Boar-helmets and forbade them peace.
    To Odin belong the earls who are slain,
      But Thor gets the kin of thralls.

THOR Unfairly would the gods fare at your hands, 25
      Were you as strong as you wish.

HARBARD You are strong enough but not stout-
              hearted,   26
    For you cowered, Thor, in the thumb of a glove
      And forgot that you were a god:
    You dared not then, your dread was so great,
    Either sneeze or fart, lest Fjalar hear.

THOR Be silent, slave! I would send you to Hel, 27
    Could I but stretch across the fjord.

HARBARD Why should you stretch? There is no strife
             between us.   28
      Meanwhile, what were you doing?

THOR I was in the east, where I held the river: 29
      There the Sons of Svarang sought me out,
      They lobbed stones but little that helped them,
      I beat them down till they begged for peace.
        Meanwhile, what were you doing?

HARBARD I was traveling in the east where I talked and
            played 30
         With a linen-white one and had a love-
            meeting:
         I gladdened Gold-bright and gave her pleasure.

THOR You had luck in your choice of a lovely maid. 31

HARBARD I could have used your help, then, to hold her
            fast. 32

THOR I would have helped you, had I had the
        chance. 33

HARBARD I would have trusted you, had you not
            betrayed our pact. 34

THOR I am no heel-biter like an old hide-shoe in
        Spring. 35

HARBARD Meanwhile, what were you doing? 36

THOR I battled in Hlesey with the Berserk's wives, 37
      Who had done their worst to bewitch the folk.

HARBARD It was base of you, Thor, to battle with
            women. 38

129

THOR   No women they were, but wolves rather: *39*
They shattered my ship on the shore where
     I beached it
And chased away Thjalfi with threatening
     clubs.
     Meanwhile, what were you doing?

HARBARD   I was with an army: hither we came   *40*
To raise banners and redden spears.

THOR   Do you mean that you came to make war?   *41*

HARBARD   A ring would better the bargain for you,   *42*
A cool umpire to calm our dispute.

THOR   From where did you take such taunting
     words?   *43*
Never have I borne with more bitter taunts.

HARBARD   I took them from men, from men of old   *44*
     Who are housed in Earth's Wood.

THOR   A goodly name you give to barrows   *45*
When you hail them as Earth's Wood.

HARBARD   Thus I judge such things.   *46*

THOR   Little good would you get for your glibness
     of tongue   *47*
     If I should wade through the water:
Louder than a wolf, I believe, you would
     presently
Howl at a tap from my hammer.

HARBARD   You could prove your mettle with more
               point at home,   48
    Where Sif in your absence sits with a lover.

THOR   What you say now is of all news the worst: 49
    Shameless coward, I am sure that you lie.

HARBARD   I say it is true: you are slow on your journey.   50
    Further would you have stepped had you
               started at dawn.

THOR   You lie! It is you who have delayed my
               journey.   5

HARBARD   I never thought that Thor of the gods   52
      Would be worsted on his way by a herdsman.

THOR   Harbard, bring your boat across now: 53
    Let us argue no more; come to Magni's
               father.

HARBARD   Depart from the fjord: your passage is
               denied.   54

THOR   Then show me the way since you won't
               ferry me.   55

HARBARD   Little it is to deny, long it is to travel: 56
    An hour to the stock, to the stone another,
    Keep left till you reach the Land of Man;
    There will Fjörgyn meet Thor, her son,
    And show him the highway to Odin's land.

THOR   Shall I reach home today?   57

HARBARD   By sunrise with much sorrow and toil   *58*
          Thor will get home, I think.

THOR   We will speak no more: if we meet again,   *59*
          You shall pay for your refusal to ferry me over.

HARBARD   Drop dead! May the demons have you!   *60*

Loki's Flyting

Aegir, who was also known as Gymir, had prepared ale for the gods, when he received the great kettle, as was told earlier. To his party came Odin and his wife Frigg. Thor did not come, for he was in the east. Sif, Thor's wife, was there, Bragi and his wife Idun. Tyr was there; he was one-handed; Fenris-wolf had bitten off his hand while being bound. There was Njörd and his wife Skadi, Frey and Freya, and Odin's son Vidar. Loki was there and Frey's servants Byggvir and Beyla. There were many gods and elves. Aegir had two servers, Fimafeng and Eldir. The ale served itself. There was a great peace in that place, all praised Aegir's servers highly. Loki could not bear to hear praise, so he killed Fimafeng. Then the gods shook their spears at Loki and cried out, driving him away to the woods; then they returned to their drinking. Loki turned back and met Eldir outside. Loki said to him:

LOKI	Stay where you are, step no further,	1
	Eldir, till you have told me	
	Of what the gods, of what the elves,	
	Are talking over their ale.	
ELDIR	They boast of their weapons, their boldness	
	in arms	2
	As they sit by the banquet-board,	
	But none of the gods, none of the elves	
	Speak of or wish you well.	
LOKI	I shall go in to eye them feasting	3
	In Aegir's banquet hall:	

I intend to stir up strife and hate,
    Mingle gall with their mead.

ELDIR　If you go in to eye them feasting　　4
    In Aegir's banquet hall
And sprinkle the gods with spite and malice,
    They will wipe your face with your words.

LOKI　I tell you, Eldir, if we two should begin　　5
    To bandy bitter words,
I should be ready with apt replies
    Were you to wag your tongue.

(*Loki enters the hall.*)

From a long journey has Loftus come　　6
    And thirsty is his throat:
I ask the gods to give me a cup,
    A great goblet of mead.

Why so silent and sullen, gods,　　7
    Too moody to speak with me?
Appoint me a seat, a place at the feast,
    Or else bid me be off.

BRAGI　An appointed seat, a place at the feast,　　8
    The gods will never give you:
You are not one they wish to invite
    As a friend to their pleasure feast.

LOKI　Remember, Odin, in the olden days　　9
    What blood-brothers we were:
You would never have dreamed of drinking ale
    Unless it was brought for us both.

ODIN Make room, Vidar, room for the Wolf's *10*
  Father to sit at our feast,
Lest Loki abuse us with bitter words
  In Aegir's banquet hall.

LOKI Hail to the gods, hail to the goddesses, *11*
  Hail to the Holy Powers,
Hail to you all, all but one,
  You, Bragi, on that bench.

BRAGI I will give you a mare, a mace also, *12*
  And, to better the bargain, a ring,
To refrain, Loki, from malicious words,
  Inciting the gods against you.

LOKI Neither horses nor arm-rings have you to
    give, *13*
  For you lack both, Bragi,
Of all who sit here, elves and gods,
  The most backward in battle,
  The shyest when arrows are shot.

BRAGI If I were outside, not sitting at table *14*
  In Aegir's banquet hall,
My arm would have your head from your neck,
  With pain repay your lies.

LOKI Boldly you speak, less boldly you act, *15*
  Bragi, the bench-ornament:
If you are angry, come out and fight,
  A hero should feel no fear.

IDUN Think, Bragi, I beg, of our children, *16*
  Of all our kith and kin

135

And do not bandy abuse with Loki
In Aegir's banquet hall.

LOKI   Enough, Idun! I know what you are,   17
         The most wanton of women:
     Once, half-washed you wound your arms
         About your brother's killer.

IDUN   I will not bandy abuse with Loki   18
         In Aegir's banquet hall:
     Be calm, Bragi, and keep the peace,
         Nor let ale rouse you to rage.

GEFJUN   Why at the table should two gods   19
         Bandy bitter words?
     Loki is envious, as we all know,
         And hates the Holy Powers.

LOKI   Enough, Gefjun! I know your secrets,   20
         I know your seducer's name,
     The white god who gave you a jewel
         To lay your leg over his.

ODIN   You are mad, Loki, you have lost your wits,   21
         To give offense to Gefjun:
     She is wise, I think, and what is to come
         Beholds as clearly as I.

LOKI   Enough, Odin! You have never been   22
         A just judge of warriors:
     You have often allowed, as allow you should not,
         Faint-hearted fighters to win.

ODIN   If I have allowed, as allow I should not,   23
         Faint-hearted fighters to win,

You lived under the earth for eight winters,
And bore babies there,
Were milked like a milch-cow
And played a woman's part.

LOKI   Charms on Samsey, they say you worked,   *24*
Wicked spells like a witch,
Flew about in the form of a wizard
And played a woman's part.

FRIGG   You are mad, Loki, to mention here,   *25*
Aloud among the living,
What befell two gods in former days,
And disdain their deeds of old.

LOKI   Enough, Frigg! You are Fjörgyn's daughter   *26*
And have ever played the whore:
Both Ve and Vili, Vidrir's wife,
You allowed to lie with you.

FRIGG   If I still had a son, sitting here,   *27*
As brave as Baldur was,
You would not escape unscathed from the hall,
Before you fought with him.

LOKI   If you like, Frigg, there's a lot more   *28*
I can tell you about my tricks:
For I saw to it that your son died,
That Baldur will not come back.

FREYA   You are mad, Loki, to mention here   *29*
Your foul and ugly arts:
Frigg knows all that is fated to be,
Though she does not say so herself.

LOKI   Enough, Freya! I know well   *30*
       You have been as bad as the rest:
With all who sit here, elves and gods,
       With each you have played the whore.

FREYA   False is your tongue. You will find before
          long   *31*
       That ill comes to the evil:
The gods are enraged, the goddesses also;
       Unhappy will you go hence.

LOKI   Enough, Freya! I know you a witch   *32*
       Who has done many wicked deeds:
You enticed into bed your own brother,
          remember,
       And then, Freya, you farted.

NJÖRD   It's a small matter if a maiden chooses   *33*
       To lie with a husband or lover,
But a shameful sight is a She-god
       Who has given birth to babies.

LOKI   Beware, Njörd! I know you were sent   *34*
       From the east as a hostage to gods:
For Hymir's daughters you did as a piss-trough,
       They made water in your mouth.

NJÖRD   It comforted me when I came from afar   *35*
       In the east as a hostage to gods,
To beget a son who is greatly loved
       And appears the prince of gods.

LOKI   Beware, Njörd! It is wise to be modest.   *36*
       Your secret I shall not conceal:

On your own sister that son you begot.
    What else would one expect?

TYR   Frey is the best of all bold riders   37
    In the golden courts of the gods,
Never dallies with maidens, nor men's wives,
    But frees all from their fetters.

LOKI   Enough, Tyr! You have never known how   38
    To make peace between men:
Feeble you are since Fenris bit
    Your right hand off at the wrist.

TYR   I lost a hand, but you lost a son,   39
    The wolf brought woe to us both:
In painful fetters shall Fenris lie
    Until the twilight of gods.

LOKI   Enough, Tyr! You know that your wife   40
    Mothered a son by me:
Nor rag nor penny were you paid for that
    In recompense, wretched one.

FREY   I see a channel and a chained wolf lying   41
    Until the twilight of gods:
Forger of lies, unless you be silent,
    That fate will fall on you next.

LOKI   With gold you bought Gymir's daughter,   42
    For her you sold your sword:
When Muspell's sons over Mirkwood ride,
    Faint shall you feel at heart.

BYGGVIR   Could I own to the lineage of Ingvi-Frey   43
    And sit in so honored a seat,

139

I would pound you, crow, to pulp for your
    words
    And break every one of your bones.

LOKI   What do I see wagging its tail   44
    And yelping like a spoiled pup?
To Frey it must sound like slave-girls'
    Jibber-jabber at the quern.

BYGGVIR   My name is Byggvir, known, I think,   45
    To all for my hot temper:
Happy am I that Hropt's kin
    Are gathered over their ale.

LOKI   Enough, Byggvir! You have never learned   46
    How to carve meat for men:
When others fought you hid yourself
    Under the straw of the hall.

HEIMDAL   Drink, Loki, has dulled your wits,   47
    It is time to leave it alone:
When ale begins to take hold of a man,
    He babbles babyish nonsense.

LOKI   Enough, Heimdal! I know that fate   48
    Assigned you a servile task;
With a damp bottom you are doomed to stay
    Awake to guard the gods.

SKADI   You are lively, Loki, but, like it or not,   49
    You will not be loose for long:
The gods will bind you to the blade of a sword
    With the guts of your ice-cold heir.

LOKI   If the gods bind me to the blade of a sword   *50*
          With the guts of my ice-cold heir,
     I was foremost at the slaughter, first to lay
          Harsh hands on Thjazi.

SKADI   If foremost at the slaughter, first to lay   *51*
          Harsh hands on Thjazi,
     Ominous words shall you hear in my temple,
          Dire prophecies on my plains.

LOKI   Livelier your words to Laufey's son   *52*
          When you bid him come to your bed:
     Now is the time for telling all,
          That must be told of too.

SIF   Hail, Loki! Let me hand you now   *53*
          A cup of cold mead:
     Admit that in one among the gods
          Even you can find no fault.

LOKI   That would be Sif, for, wary ever   *54*
          And cautious, you kept to yourself,
     Except that you lay with a lover once
          As well as Thor, I think,
          And the lucky one was Loki.

BEYLA   The fells tremble, the fields shake,   *55*
          That must be Thor returning:
     He will surely smite the shameless mocker
          Of gods and the sons of gods.

LOKI   Enough, Beyla! You are Byggvir's wife   *56*
          And mingle in much evil:
     A disgrace it is that where gods sit
          Such a dung-bird and coward should come.

(*Thor enters.*)

THOR   Be silent and grovel, or my great hammer   57
         Mjöllnir shall shut your mouth:
     Your shoulder's stone I will strike from its neck,
         Lifeless you shall lie.

LOKI   So! The Son of Earth is here at last!   58
         Why do you rant and rage?
     Less bold you will be when you battle with
         Fenris
     And he swallows Odin whole.

THOR   Be silent and grovel, or my great hammer   59
         Mjöllnir shall shut your mouth:
     Be silent or Thor will throw you to the East
         Where no god shall see you again.

LOKI   Of your eastward journey, if I were you,   60
         I would not speak before warriors:
     You cowered, Thor, in the thumb of a glove,
         And forgot that you were a god.

THOR   Be silent and grovel, or my great hammer   61
         Mjöllnir shall shut your mouth:
     My hand will fell you with Hrungnir's-killer,
         Break every one of your bones.

LOKI   I reckon I shall live to a ripe old age   62
         For all your threats with the hammer:
     Skrymir's straps were strong, you found,
         When you could not get to your gear
         And almost died of hunger.

THOR   Be silent and grovel, or my great hammer   *63*
        Mjöllnir shall shut your mouth:
        I will send you to Hel with Hrungnir's-killer,
        Down to the gates of the dead.

LOKI   I have said to gods and the sons of gods   *64*
        What my mind was amused to say:
        But now I shall go, for I know your rages,
        With Thor I'm afraid to fight.

        Ale have you brewed, Aegir, but never   *65*
        Will you give a feast again:
        My flames play over all you possess,
        Already they burn your back.

*   *   *

But after that Loki hid in Franang's Falls in the form of a salmon. There the gods took him. He was bound with the bowels of his son Nari. But his son Narfi turned into a wolf. Skadi took a poison snake and hung it up over the face of Loki; the poison dropped down. Sigyn, Loki's wife, sat there and held a bowl under the poison, and when the bowl was full she carried it off; but, meanwhile, the poison dropped on Loki. Then he struggled so hard that all the earth trembled. We call that now an earthquake.

Song of the Sybil

Heidi men call me when their homes I visit,　　　　*1*
A far-seeing witch, wise in talismans,
Caster of spells, cunning in magic,
To wicked women welcome always.

Arm-rings and necklaces, Odin, you gave me　　　　*2*
To learn my lore, to learn my magic:
Wider and wider through all worlds I see.

Outside I sat by myself when you came,　　　　*3*
Terror of the Gods, and gazed in my eyes.
What do you ask of me? Why tempt me?
Odin, I know where your eye is concealed,
Hidden away in the Well of Mimir:
Mimir each morning his mead drinks
From Valfather's Pledge. *Well, would you know
　　　more?*

Of Heimdal, too, and his horn I know,　　　　*4*
Hidden under the holy tree;
Down on it pours a precious stream
From Valfather's Pledge. *Well, would you know
　　　more?*

Silence I ask of the Sacred Folk,　　　　*5*
Silence of the kith and kin of Heimdal:
At your will, Valfather, I shall well relate
The old songs of men I remember best.

I tell of giants from times forgotten,   *6*
Those who fed me in former days:
Nine Worlds I can reckon, nine roots of the Tree,
The wonderful Ash, way under the ground.

When Ymir lived long ago   *7*
Was no sand or sea, no surging waves,
Nowhere was there earth nor heaven above,
But a grinning gap and grass nowhere.

The Sons of Bur then built up the lands,   *8*
Molded in magnificence Middle Earth:
Sun stared from the south on the stones of their hall,
From the ground there sprouted green leeks.

Sun turned from the south, Sister of Moon,   *9*
Her right arm rested on the rim of Heaven;
She had no inkling where her hall was,
Nor Moon a notion of what might be had,
The planets knew not where their places were.

The High Gods gathered in council   *10*
In their Hall of Judgment, all the rulers:
To Night and to Nightfall their names gave,
The Morning they named and the Mid-Day,
Mid-Winter, Mid-Summer, for the assigning of
    years.

At Idavale the Aesir met: *11*
Temple and altar they timbered and raised,
Set up a forge to smithy treasures,
Tongs they fashioned and tools wrought;

Played chess in the court and cheerful were;   *12*
Gold they lacked not, the gleaming metal.

Then came Three, the Thurse Maidens,
Rejoicing in their strength, from Gianthome.

The High Gods gathered in council   13
In their Hall of Judgment: Who of the dwarves
Should mold man by mastercraft
From Brimir's blood and Bláin's limbs?

Mótsognir was their mighty ruler,   14
Greatest of dwarves, and Durin after him:
The dwarves did as Durin directed,
Many man-forms made from the earth.

Nýi and Nídi, Nordri, Sudri,   15
Austri and Vestri, Althjóf, Dvalin,
Bívor, Bávor, Bömbur, Nóri,
An and Ánar, Óinn, Mjödvitnir,
Veig and Gandálf, Vindálf, Thorin,
Thrór and Thráin, Thekkur, Littur,
Vitur, Nyr and Nýrádur,
Fíli, Kíli, Fundin, Náli,
Hefti, Víli, Hanar, Svíur,
Billing, Brúni, Bíldur, and Buri,
Frár, Hornbori, Fraegur, Lóni,
Aurvangur, Jari, Eikinskjaldi:
(All Durin's folk I have duly named.)

I must tell of the dwarves in Dvalin's host;   16
Like lions they were in Lokar's time:
In Juravale's marsh they made their dwelling,
From their stone hall set out on journeys.

There was Draupnir and Dólgthrasir,   17
Hár, Haugspori, Hlévangur, Glói,
Dori, Ori, Dufur, Andvari,

146

Skirfir, Virfir, Skáfidur, Ái,
Álf and Yngvi, Eikinskjaldi,
Fjalar and Frosti, Finn and Ginnar:
Men will remember while men live
The long line of Lofar's forebears.

Then from the host Three came,   *18*
Great, merciful, from the god's home:
Ash and *Elm* on earth they found,
Faint, feeble, with no fate assigned them.

Breath they had not, nor blood nor senses,   *19*
Nor language possessed, nor life-hue:
Odin gave them breath, Haenir senses,
Blood and life-hue Lodur gave.

I know an ash-tree, named Yggdrasil: *20*
Sparkling showers are shed on its leaves
That drip dew into the dales below.
By Urd's Well it waves evergreen,
Stands over that still pool,
Near it a bower whence now there come
The Fate Maidens, first Urd.
Skuld second, scorer of runes,
Then Verdandi, third of the Norns:
The laws that determine the lives of men
They fixed forever and their fate sealed.

The first war in the world I well remember,   *21*
When Gullveg was spitted on spear points
And burned in the hall of the High God:
Thrice burned, thrice reborn
Often laid low, she lives yet.

147

The gods hastened to their Hall of Judgment,   22
Sat in council to decide whether
To endure great loss in loud strife
Or let both command men's worship.

At the host Odin hurled his spear   23
In the first world-battle; broken was the plankwall
Of the god's fortress: the fierce Vanes
Caused war to occur in the fields.

The gods hastened to their Hall of Judgment,   24
Sat in council to discover who
Had tainted all the air with corruption
And Odin's Maid offered to the giants.

One Thor felled in his fierce rage;   25
Seldom he sits when of such he hears:
Oaths were broken, binding vows,
Solemn agreements sworn between them.

Valkyries I saw, coming from afar,   26
Eagerly riding to aid the Goths;
Skuld bore one shield, Skögul another,
Gunn, Hild, Göngul and Spearskögul:
Duly have I named the Daughters of Odin,
The valiant riders, the Valkyries.

Baldur I saw, the bleeding god,   27
His fate still hidden, Odin's son:
Tall on the plain a plant grew,
A slender marvel, the mistletoe.

From that fair shrub, shot by Hödur,   28
Flew the fatal dart that felled the God,

But Baldur's Brother was born soon after:
Though one night old, Odin's Son
Took a vow to avenge that death.

His hands he washed not nor his hair combed   *29*
Till Baldur's Bane was borne to the pyre:
Deadly the bow drawn by Vali,
The strong string of stretched gut,
But Frigg wept in Fensalir
For the woe of Valhalla. *Well, would you know
    more?*

I see one in bonds by the boiling springs;   *30*
Like Loki he looks, loathsome to view:
There Sigyn sits, sad by her husband,
In woe by her man. *Well, would you know more?*

From the east through Venom Valley runs   *31*
Over jagged rocks the River Gruesome.

North, in Darkdale, stands the dwelling place   *32*
Of Sindri's kin, covered with gold;
A hall also in Everfrost,
The banquet hall of Brimir the Giant.

A third I see, that no sunlight reaches,   *33*
On Dead Man's Shore: the doors face northward,
Through its smoke vent venom drips,
Serpent skins enskein that hall.

Men wade there, tormented by the stream,   *34*
Vile murderers, men forsworn,
And artful seducers of other men's wives:
Nidhögg sucks blood from the bodies of the dead,
The Wolf rends them. *Well, would you know more?*

In the east dwells a crone, in Ironwood: *35*
The brood of Fenris are bred there,
Wolf-monsters, one of whom
Eventually shall devour the sun.

The giant's Watchman, joyful Eggthur, *36*
Sits on his howe and harps well:
The red cock, called All-Knower
Boldly crows from Birdwood.

Goldencomb to the Gods crows, *37*
Who wakes the warriors in Valhalla:
A soot-red hen also calls
From Hel's Hall, deep under the ground.

Loud howls Garm before Gnipahellir, *38*
Bursting his fetters, Fenris runs:
Further in the future, afar I behold
The Twilight of the gods who gave victory.

Brother shall strike brother and both fall, *39*
Sisters' sons slay each other,
Evil be on earth, an Age of Whoredom,
Of sharp sword-play and shields' clashing,
A Wind-Age, a Wolf-Age, till the world ruins:
No man to another shall mercy show.

The waters are troubled, the waves surge up: *40*
Announcing now the knell of Fate,
Heimdal winds his horn aloft,
On Hel's Road all men tremble.

Yggdrasil trembles, the towering Ash *41*
Groans in woe; the Wolf is loose:

Odin speaks with the Head of Mimir
Before he is swallowed by Surt's kin.

From the east drives Hrym, lifts up his shield,   *42*
The squamous serpent squirms with rage,
The Great Worm with the waves contending,
The pale-beaked eagle pecks at the dead,
Shouting for joy : the ship Naglfar

Sails out from the east, at its helm Loki,   *43*
With the children of darkness, the doom-bringers,
Offspring of monsters, allies of the Wolf,
All who Byleist's Brother follow.

What of the gods? What of the elves?   *44*
Gianthome groans, the gods are in council,
The dwarves grieve before their door of stone,
Masters of walls. *Well, would you know more?*

Surt with the bane-of-branches comes   *45*
From the south, on his sword the sun of the Valgods,
Crags topple, the crone falls headlong,
Men tread Hel's Road, the Heavens split open.

A further woe falls upon Hlín   *46*
As Odin comes forth to fight the Wolf;
The killer of Beli battles with Surt :
Now shall fall Frigg's beloved.

Now valiant comes Valfather's Son,   *47*
Vidar, to vie with Valdyr in battle,
Plunges his sword into the Son of Hvedrung,
Avenging his father with a fell thrust.

Now the Son of Hlödyn and Odin comes   *48*
To fight with Fenris; fiercest of warriors,
He mauls in his rage all Middle Earth;
Men in fear all flee their homesteads;
Nine paces back steps Bur's Son,
Retreats from the Worm, of taunts unafraid.

Now death is the portion of doomed men,   *49*
Red with blood the buildings of gods,
The sun turns black in the summer after,
Winds whine. *Well, would you know more?*

Earth sinks in the sea, the sun turns black,   *50*
Cast down from Heaven are the hot stars,
Fumes reek, into flames burst,
The sky itself is scorched with fire.

I see Earth rising a second time   *51*
Out of the foam, fair and green;
Down fron the fells, fish to capture,
Wings the eagle; waters flow.

At Idavale the Aesir meet: *52*
They remember the Worm of Middle Earth,
Ponder again the Great Twilight
And the ancient runes of the High God.

Boards shall be found of a beauty to wonder at,   *53*
Boards of gold in the grass long after,
The chess boards they owned in the olden days.

Unsown acres shall harvests bear,   *54*
Evil be abolished, Baldur return
And Hropt's Hall with Hödur rebuild,
Wise gods. *Well, would you know more?*

Haenir shall wield the wand of prophecy,   55
The sons of two brothers set up their dwelling
In wide Windhome. *Well, would you know more?*

Fairer than sunlight, I see a hall,   56
A hall thatched with gold in Gimlé:
Kind lords shall live there in delight for ever.

Now rides the Strong One to Rainbow Door,   57
Powerful from heaven, the All-Ruler:
From the depths below a drake comes flying,
The Dark Dragon from Darkfell,
Bears on his pinions the bodies of men,
Soars overhead. I sink now.

Notes

The Words of the High One

Many critics divide the 'Words' (*Hávamál*) into six parts, but we have felt that five sections better retain what we consider the 'sense' of the original. These are: strophes 1–82, the 'Words of the High One' in the strictest sense; 83–96, the tale of Odin and Billing's daughter; 97–104, the tale of how Odin got the mead of poetry; 105–129, the *Lodd-fafnismál*, wisdom much like that of the first part; and 130–157, the tale of how Odin won the runes and the tabulation of the runes (these are sometimes considered separate sections).

3 This seems to be the Icelandic equivalent of 'clothes make the man', but we have altered a good deal to get this reading.

107–129 Most of the verses reproduce the lines of 106; we have here elided the repetition.

128 This is a most difficult strophe. It seems to read: Strong is the beam which must be raised/ To give entrance to all:/ Give it a ring, or grim deeds/ Will be gotten by you. We have interpreted this 'ring' as a good-luck charm, rather than a structural member of the doorway. The strophe thus describes a custom akin to hanging a horseshoe at an entry.

The Lay of Grimnir

4 *Land of Strength*: Thrudheim, the place where Thor has his hall, Bilskirnir. Cf. 24.

1–7 *Tooth-fee*: a reference to the custom of giving a child a gift when he cuts his first tooth. It is still in vogue in Iceland.

6 *Hall of the Dead*: Odin's home. Perhaps identical to the 'Sunk-Bench' of strophe 7 and the 'Glad-Home' of 8.

12 Baldur's home is free from everything unclean.

13 Heimdal's home is at the end of Bifröst, the rainbow bridge.

15 We know nothing of Forseti save that Snorri says that he was 'the son of Baldur and Nanna. . . . All who come to him with difficult cases to settle go away satisfied. He is the best judge among gods and men'.

18 Each day the gods' cook (Sooty-Face) cooks the flesh of the boar (Soot-of-the-Sea) in the great kettle (Sooty-with-fire). The boar's flesh suffices for all the warriors and he is resurrected each evening to be cooked again the next morning.

19 Odin gives his share of the boar to two wolves (Greedy and Grim), as wine is food and drink enough for him.

21 The fish of the wolf is the sun, caught and devoured at Ragnarök by the wolf, Skoll (cf. 'Song of the Sybil').

22 Gate-of-Dead is the outer gate of Valhalla.

26 Oak-Thorn (= antlered) is usually considered to embody the clouds.

27–35 Many scholars consider these enumerative strophes an interpolation. The names vary from manuscript to manuscript.

29 Snorri tells us that Yggdrasil's third root 'stands in heaven and beneath this root is a spring called Urd's Well'. . . . There the gods have their judgment seat to which they ride each day over Bifröst. . . .' Nothing is known of the rivers in this strophe.

31 It is hard to reconcile this with the information in strophe 29. Some editors consider the root of 29 to be the second one enumerated here.

33 and 34 Nothing is known of the harts or the serpents mentioned here.

36 The list of Valkyrie names given here differs in many respects from that of 'Song of the Sybil'.

40 This passage parallels that in the 'Lay of Vafthrudnir'.

42 *Invaldi* is the progenitor of all craftsmen-dwarves.

45–48 Little is known of most of these by-names of Odin (e.g. Thud and Ud), though some (e.g. Traveler, Warrior, or Third — Snorri tells us of a tripartite deity High, Equally-High, and Third) are fairly simple.

49 Nothing is known of this episode. It may be noted here that the German scholar Genzmer silently elides seventeen strophes from this poem — thus eliminating many problems.

53 *Skilfing*: literally 'The Shaker'.

The Lay of Vafthrudnir

13, 15, 17 The strophes begin with the first two lines of 11, which we have here deleted.

18 *Rasts*, a unit of measurement customarily translated 'miles'. Actually the unit seems to have varied. *Röst* means 'resting place' and in rough terrain these came more frequently than in smooth. An immense distance is usually given as 'a hundred rasts', as here.

22, 24, 26, etc. These strophes all have 'If your wisdom serves you well' as second line. We have again deleted the repetition.

49 *Maidens in threes.* . . . It has been suggested that these are Norns, but as there is no mention elsewhere of an

alternate set of Norns, this seems unlikely. More probably, they are Valkyries.

54 As remarked in the Introduction, Odin here cheats his opponent. A similar 'non-riddle' is used by Bilbo Baggins in J. R. R. Tolkien's *The Hobbit*.

The Words of the All-Wise

(In several verses we have sacrificed alliteration to retain the names of the things enumerated.)

1 The 'bride' here mentioned seems to be Thrud (might), the only one of Thor's daughters whose name is recorded. Her mother was Sif.

2 *White-Nose*. The dwarves lived out of the sun's light and were therefore pale.

11, 13, 15, etc. The first line of strophe 9 is repeated at the head of each query. Again we have deleted the repetitions.

24 and 32 Note that the elves have the same name for *the sea* and *brew*. There has been much discussion of this. Perhaps the best solution is that the elves thought of all 'water-like' liquids that did not taste like water as 'charmed water'.

35 Note how different Thor's and Odin's tricks are.

The Lay of Thrym

1 The *sacred Hammer* is, of course, Mjöllnir.

10 The *Brising Necklace* is sometimes assigned to Frigg and sometimes to Freya.

The Lay of Hymir

5 It is not known just why Tyr, the son of Odin, here refers to Hymir as his father.

7 Thor is usually pictured driving a chariot pulled by two goats: Tooth-grinder and Gat-Tooth.

11 While Hrod's foe is Thor, nothing is known of Hrod.

19 Hymir is Brother of Apes because Ape = Fool and giants were thought of as stupid.

25 *Sea-buck* is a kenning for ship. Cf. *sea-stallion* in strophe 26.

31 The actual reading of line 4 is doubtful.

36 Snorri puts the blame for the laming of one of Thor's goats on the son of the farmer, not on Loki.

The Lay of Erik

This is one of the many Skaldic poems not included in the *Edda*. It is preserved in only one manuscript, the so-called *Fagrskinna* ('Beautiful-Skin'). It was supposedly written at the request of Gunnhild, wife of Erik Blood-Axe, after he was killed at the battle of Stainmore in 954.

11 These are the five kings killed with Erik at Stainmore. The incident is described in the *Saga of Hákon the Good*, chapter 4.

The Treachery of Asmund

This non-*Eddic* poem is found in *Halfs saga*, one of the *fornaldarsögur*, or 'tales of olden times'.

8 *Hair-hills* is a kenning for 'heads'.

16 *Hawks* is a kenning for 'warriors'.
   Swords were coated with wax to prevent rusting and guard against witchcraft.

20 Furnishers of rings are princes or battle-chiefs; here Half is meant.

22 Odin is the All-Father.

The Waking of Angantyr

This non-*Eddic* poem is found in the *Saga of King Heidrek the Wise*. We have added strophe 1 from the version in the *Hauksbók* manuscript.

14 *Tyrfing*. Svafrlami forced Dvalin and Dulinn to forge him a sword which had a hilt and handle of gold, which would never rust, and which would cut iron as though it were cloth. The dwarves forged the sword, but Dvalin cursed it, saying that it would kill a man each time it was drawn, and that it would perform three dastardly deeds, as well as be the cause of Svafrlami's death. Arngrim then took Svafrlami's daughter and had twelve sons by her. Angantyr, the eldest, fell heir to Tyrfing. Hjalmar the Haughty and Arrow-Odd (the 'two who live') slew all twelve in a fight in which Hjalmar was also slain ('only one owned it later'). Odd buried the brothers in barrows with their weapons. Svava, Angantyr's wife, gave birth to a daughter (Hervor) who was inclined to fighting and weapons. Posing as a man (Hervrad) she joined a band of vikings and came thus to Munarvag.

22 *Bane of Shields*, *Hater of Byrnies*, and *Hjalmar's Killer* are all kennings for Tyrfing.

29 *Measurer of Fate* is another kenning for Tyrfing.

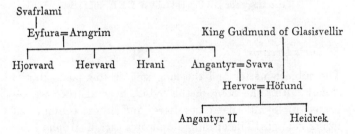

Genealogy for WAKING of ANGANTYR

The Lay of Völund

15 *Grani's Road* is the Rhine.

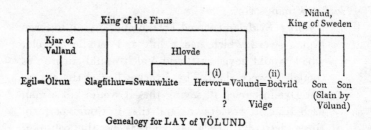

Genealogy for LAY of VÖLUND

Brunhild's Hel-Ride

8 *Tree-Foe* is a kenning for fire.
9 *Fafnir's Hoard* is the Rhine gold.

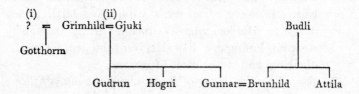

Genealogy for BRUNHILD'S HEL-RIDE

Baldur's Dreams

The subject-matter and the language of this poem link it closely with 'The Song of the Sybil'. Several lines are repeated in 'Sybil' that occur here, and others contain but minor changes. The opening duplicates part of strophe 11 of 'The Lay of Thrym'.

2 The *Hound of Hel* is Garm.

7 *The branch* was a sprig of mistletoe.

Skirnir's Ride

4 The *Glory of Elves* is the sun.

19 The apple was the Icelandic symbol of fruitfulness.

21 Odin's arm-ring ('bracelet') *Draupnir* (dropper) was fabricated for him by the dwarves.

26 What we have rendered 'Orcs' is obscure. Some editors read 'vile things'.

The Lay of Harbard

The meter of this poem is, to say the least, erratic. While much of it is in *málaháttr* (see Introduction), some lines cannot be classified under any known meter — they are simply prose, not verse. The poem is simply abuse, the opposing figures being Thor and Odin (in the guise of the ferryman).

Loki's Flyting

Many of the anecdotes mentioned by Loki are unfathomable and not mentioned elsewhere in the Scandinavian mythological fragments preserved. A notable exception is the tale of Thor's trip to the land of the giants, and the way in which he was outwitted by Utgard-Loki, their king, which Snorri tells in full (chapters 44–47). Similarly, many of the names do not occur elsewhere.

Song of the Sybil

3 The *Terror of the Gods* is Odin.

4 *Valfather's Pledge* is Odin's Eye, which he gave to

Mimir in exchange for wisdom. Mimir set it in a goblet from which he drinks his mead.

12 Actually chess was most likely not played in ancient Scandinavia; some form of backgammon is more probable (cf. strophe 53).

20 Runes were carved in wood for purposes of divination.

21 The battle between the Aesir and the Vanes almost certainly has its origin in an historical battle between Vane-worshiping tribes of the South Baltic and Aesir-worshiping Norsemen. Later the pantheons merged with an interchange of deities.

24 Loki was responsible for tainting the air.
Freya is Odin's maid.

25 I.e., Thor felled one of the giants.

29 *Baldur's Bane* is the mistletoe.

32 *Sindri's kin* are the dwarves.

35 The *crone* is the mother of two wolves, Skoll and Hati, who will respectively swallow the sun and the moon.

40 Heimdal's horn is the signal that Asgard has been invaded.

45 *Bane of branches* is a kenning for fire.

57 The *Strong One* is the resurrected Baldur.

Glossary of Names

AEGIR   god of the sea.

AESIR   group of gods to which Odin and Thor belong.

AGNAR

(in 'Brunhild's Hel-Ride')   brother of Auda. He is also mentioned in the *Sigrdrifumál*.

(in 'Lay of Grimnir')   son of Geirrod.

ALVIS   a dwarf. Literally 'All-knowing'.

ANGANTYR   a king of the Goths.

ARNGRIM   father of Angantyr and his brothers, husband of Eyfura.

ASGARD   the realm of the gods.

ASMUND'S HALL   unknown save for Grimnir 48.

ASVID   literally 'Aesir-wood', or, assuming a scribal error for *Asvit, 'God-Knowing'. Probably a giant. Unknown elsewhere.

AURGELMIR   the Frost-Giant's name for Ymir.

BALDUR'S BROTHER   Vali.

BARRI   literally, 'The Leafy'.

BELI   a giant killed by Frey.

BERGEIMIR   one of the giants who survived the flood when Ymir was slain.

BERSERKS   warriors full of the glory of battle; impervious to wounds.

BESTLA   Odin's mother.

BEYLA   servant of Frey.

BIFRÖST   the Rainbow Bridge which connects Midgard with Asgard.

163

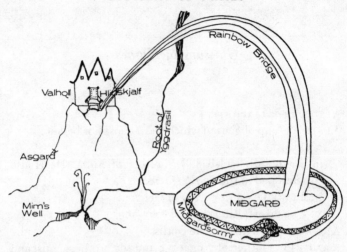

BILLING'S DAUGHTER   unknown save for 'Words of the High One'.

BILSKIRNIR   Thor's house.

BIRDWOOD   perhaps a by-name of Yggdrasil.

BLÁIN   perhaps a by-name of Ymir.

BODVILD   daughter of Nidud; seduced by Völund.

BOLTHOR   Odin's grandfather.

BOLVERK   Odin.

BRAGI   god of poetry, married to Idun.

BRIMIR   by-name of Ymir?

BRISING NECKLACE   a fabulous necklace, fabricated by the dwarves (brising = twiner) and occasionally assigned to Frigg, rather than Freya.

BRUNHILD   Valkyrie and princess.

BUDLI   father of Atli (= Attila the Hun) and Brunhild.

BUR   Odin's father, husband of Bestla.

BYGGVIR   a servant to the gods.

BYLEIST'S BROTHER   Loki.

COILER   the Midgard-Serpent.

DAIN   an elf-king.

DELLING   literally 'day-spring', the husband of Night and the father of Day.

DURIN   a dwarf-king.

DVALIN   a dwarf-king.

EGGTHUR   the giants' watchman.

EGIL   father of Thjalfi, Thor's servant.

ELDIR   one of Aegir's servants.

ELF-CANDLE   the sun.

ELIVAGUR   perhaps the Milky Way.

ERIK   Erik Blood-Axe, killed in England about the middle of the tenth century.

EYFURA   Svafrlami's daughter, Arngrim's wife. Also known as Svava. Mother of twelve sons and a daughter.

FAFNIR'S HOARD   the Rhine-gold.

FELL-DWELLER   the giant Aegir.

FENRIS   the wolf who bears Skoll and Hati — who devour the sun and moon at Ragnarök. He is the son of Loki and his capture cost Tyr his hand. (The nominative of the name is actually Fenrir; we have here used the genitive.)

FENSALIR   Frigg's hall.

FIMAFENG   one of Aegir's servants; slain by Loki.

FIMBUL-FAMBI   a bungler, a fool.

FITJUNG   the Earth; Fitjung's sons are men.

FJALAR THE WISE   another name for the giant Suttung.

FJOLVER   unknown elsewhere.

FJÖRGYN   Jord, 'Earth', Thor's mother.

FORSETI   the son of Baldur and Nanna, the 'best judge among gods and men'.

FRANANG'S FALLS   the waterfall wherein Loki hides in the guise of a salmon.

FREY   son of Njörd; chief fertility god.

FREYA   daughter of Njörd; female counterpart of Frey.

FRIGG   Odin's wife.

FROST GIANTS   sworn enemies of the gods.

FULLA   Frigg's handmaid.

GAGNRAD   literally 'gain-counsellor'.

GARM   the hound that guards Hel's realm.

GEFJUN   the goddess of those women who die maidens.

GEIRROD   evil king; slain by Odin.

GERD   a beautiful giantess; beloved of Frey.

GIMLÉ   the Hall of the Blessed.

GJUKI   father of Gunnar, Högni and Gudrun.

GNIPAHELLIR   literally 'cliff-cave'.

GRANI   Brunhild's steed.

GRANI'S ROAD   the Rhine.

GREEDY and GRIM   two wolves.

GRIMNIR   Odin, the grim one.

GUDRUN   daughter of Gjuki, sister of Gunnar and Högni (Wagner's Gutrune in *Götterdämmerung*).

GULLVEG   the first of the vanes to come among the gods. Her ill-treatment seems to have been the immediate cause of the war.

GUNNLOD   the daughter of the giant Suttung.

GYMIR = Aegir; his daughter is Gerd (see 'Skirnir's Ride').

HABROK   unknown save for 'Grimnir'.

HAENIR   the god given as hostage to the Vanes in exchange for Njörd.

HALF   famous sea-king and leader of a Viking band. After eighteen years of Viking life he visits his stepfather Asmund, who has ruled in Half's absence.

HAR   Odin, the high one.

HARBARD   literally 'Gray-beard' = Odin.

HEIDI   the sybil or seeress of 'Song of the Sybil', raised from the dead by Odin.

HEIDREK   Norse king famous for his wisdom.

HEIMDAL   watchman of the gods.

HERVARD   brother of Angantyr, his name is assumed by Hervor.

HERVOR

(in 'Waking of Angantyr')   daughter of Angantyr.

(in 'Völund')   beloved of Völund, a swan-maiden.

HILD   a Valkyrie name, literally 'fighter'.

HJALMAR   Hjalmar the Haughty, slain by Angantyr in his last battle.

HJALM-GUNNAR   a Gothic king.

HJORVARD   brother of Angantyr.

HLADGUD   a swan-maiden.

HLEBARD   a giant.

HLESEY   literally 'the island of the Sea God', Hler = Aegir.

HLIDSKJÁLF   Odin's high seat.

HLIN   Frigg.

HLÖDYN   Jord.

HLOVDE   father of Hervor.

HLYMDALE   literally, 'the valley of tumult'.

HODDMIMIR'S WOOD   Yggdrasil, which is frequently referred to as Mimir's Tree.

HÖD or HÖDUR   the blind slayer of Baldur.

HRAESVELG   the eagle which sits on the edge of the world and causes the winds with its wings.

HRANI   brother of Angantyr.

HRAUDUNG   Geirrod's father, Agnar's grandfather.

HREIDGOTHS   literally 'Riding-Goths'.

HRIDVITNIR   the mighty wolf, Fenris.

HRIMGRIMIR   a giant, literally 'Frost-Shrouded'.

HRIMNIR   a frost-giant.

167

HROD a giant.

HROK there were two Hrok's in Hlaf's host: Hrok the White and Hrok the Black. There is no way of knowing which is meant here.

HROPTATYR-ODIN either 'the crying god', or 'the prophesying god' or 'the god of the dead'.

HROPT'S HALL Valhalla; Odin's Hall.

HRUNGNIR a giant who wagered with Odin; he lost and was killed by Thor.

HRYM the leader of the giants, helmsman of Naglfar.

THE HURLER Thor.

HVEDRUNG by-name of Fenris.

HVERGELMIR a spring, the source of all rivers.

HYMIR a giant.

IDAVALE literally 'Field of Tides'.

IDUN goddess who guards the golden apples of youth.

IFING unknown elsewhere.

IM'S FATHER nothing is known of a son of Vafthrudnir.

INGVI-FREY a conflation of the German name (Ingw) used for Frey, and his Scandinavian name.

INNSTEIN son of Alf of Horthaland (Half's foremost adviser).

INVALDI father of the craftsmen-dwarves.

IRONWOOD unknown elsewhere.

JALK by-name of Odin.

JURAVALE unexplained.

LAERAD'S BOUGHS presumably the twigs of Yggdrasil.

LAUFEY mother of Loki.

LIF mother of the new race.

LIFTHRASNIR father of the new race; consort of Lif. Their names may mean 'Life' and 'Strong Life'.

LODDFAFNIR   a *skáld*.

LODUR   probably another name for Loki.

LOFAR   one of the primeval dwarves.

LOKI   evilest and most mischievous of the gods.

LONGBEARD   by-name of Odin.

MAGNI   son of Thor and the giantess Jarnsaxa. Together
with his brother Modi he inherits Mjöllnir.

MEILI   a virtually unknown son of Odin.

MIDVITNIR'S SON   presumably Sokkmimir.

MIMIR   a wise water-spirit.

MIRKWOOD   a magic, dark forest.

MISKURBLINDI   unknown, sometimes this line is trans-
lated 'Like a blinded man he seemed', but this is with-
out foundation.

MJÖLLNIR   Thor's magic hammer.

MODI   brother of Magni.

MOGTHRASNIR   literally 'desiring sons'. Unknown else-
where.

MÓTSOGNIR   a dwarf.

MUNARVAG   mythical place-name in 'Angantyr'.

MUNDILFERI   literally 'The Turner', father of the Sun
and the Moon.

MUSPELL'S SONS   the denizens of the realm of fire.

NAGLFAR   the ship of the giants, made of the finger-nails
of the dead.

NARFI   son of Loki.

NARI   son of Loki.

NIDHÖGG   the dragon which gnaws at the roots of Ygg-
drasil.

NIDUD   king of the Njars; father of Bodvild and two sons,
slain by Völund.

NJARS   an eastern people.

169

NJÖRD   chief of the Vanes; father of Frey and Freya.

NOATUN   'ships' haven'. Njörd's home.

NÖR   a giant.

ODIN   chief of the gods.

ODRERIR   the name of the magic mead of poetry (in *Words* 132 it seems to be the mead's container; we have altered this).

RADSEY   literally 'Isle of Counsel'.

RAGNARÖK   destruction-of-the-gods.

RATI   gimlet with which Odin bored his way into Suttung's hall.

RINDUR   mother of Vali.

RIVER GRUESOME   unknown elsewhere.

ROGALAND   port in Denmark.

SAEVERSTOD   literally 'Sea-Stead'.

SAGA   perhaps another name for Frigg, though Snorri considers her a separate goddess.

SAMSEY   perhaps the Danish island of Samsö.

SIF   Thor's wife.

SIGMUND   the most famous of all the Germanic heroes.

SIGYN   Loki's wife.

SINDRI   a dwarf.

SINFJOTLI   son of Sigmund.

SKADI   Njörd's wife, the daughter of the giant Thjazi.

SKATALUND   literally 'Warrior's Grove'.

SKIDBLADNIR   a ship, built by the craftsmen-dwarves, which always had a fair wind, and which could be folded up and stored in a pocket.

SKIRNIR   Frey's servant.

SKÖGUL   a Valkyrie.

SKOLDINGS descendants of a mythical king who was said to be Odin's son; the Danes.

SKRYMIR a giant, Snorri tells of Thor's encounter with him on a visit to Jötunheim.

SKULD this name occurs twice, once obviously referring to one of the Norns (literally 'Shall-Be'), and once to one of the Valkyries.

SLEIPNIR Odin's magic steed; it is grey and has eight legs.

SOKKMIMIR Midvitnir's son.

SURT a giant who rules the realm of fire, Muspellheim.

SUTTUNG a giant.

SVAFRLAMI grandson of Odin.

SVARANG a giant.

THAKRAD Nidud's servant.

THJALFI Thor's servant.

THJAZI a giant.

THJODRERIR a dwarf; unknown save for 'Words of the High One'.

THOUGHT and MEMORY the names of Odin's two ravens.

THRUDGELMIR a giant.

THRYM a frost-giant.

THUND Odin.

THURSE giant; Thurse maidens are giantesses.

TOFA Svava, Angantyr's wife.

TYR god of battle.

TYRFING see note to 'Angantyr', 14.

ULL son of Sif and god of archery.

URD'S WELL Urd, 'the Past', is one of the three Norns; her well irrigates Yggdrasil.

UTSTEIN Innstein's younger brother.

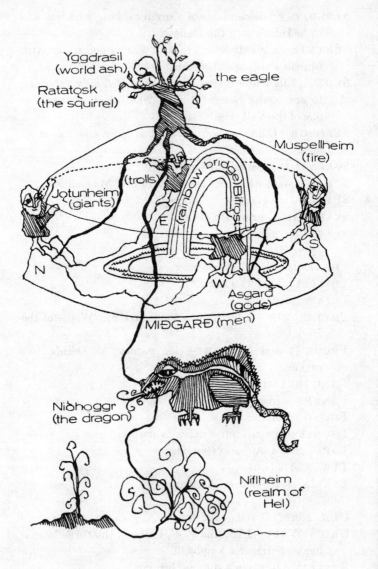

VAFTHRUDNIR   literally 'Mighty in Riddles'.

VALDYR   literally 'Beast of the Slain'.

VALFATHER   Odin.

VALGODS   the Aesir.

VALI   son of Rindur and Odin; begotten specifically to avenge Baldur's death.

VANAHEIM   the residence of the Vanes.

VE   brother of Odin.

VENOM VALLEY   mythical place-name.

VERDANDI   'the Present', one of the Norns.

VEUR   Thor.

VIDAR   Odin's son; second in strength to Thor.

VIDRIR   Odin.

VIGRID   literally, 'the field of battle'.

VILI   Odin's brother.

VING-THOR   Thor the Hurler.

VÖLUND   master smith; equivalent to the classical Daedalus.

YGG   Odin.

YGGDRASIL   the world ash (see cosmographical diagram, opposite).

YMIR   the frost giant, of whose body the world was made.